THE AMERICAN EXPLORATION AND TRAVEL SERIES

THE ROAD TO VIRGINIA CITY

THE ROAD TO

VIRGINIA CITY *The Diary of James Knox Polk Miller*

Edited by Andrew Rolle

NORMAN AND LONDON : UNIVERSITY OF OKLAHOMA PRESS

by Andrew Rolle

An American in California (San Marino, California, 1956)

The Road to Virginia City: The Diary of James Knox Polk Miller (editor) (Norman, 1960)

The Lost Cause: The Confederate Exodus to Mexico (Norman, 1965)

The Immigrant Upraised: Italian Adventures and Colonists in an Expanding America (Norman, 1968)

The Italian Americans: Troubled Roots (Norman, 1984)

Library of Congress Catalog Card Number: 60–8750
ISBN: 0–8061–2163–7

The Road to Virginia City: The Diary of James Knox Polk Miller is Volume 30 in The American Exploration and Travel Series.

TO ROSS TOOLE

Who first saw the significance of the Miller diary

CONTENTS

ILLUSTRATIONS

MAP

xi

EDITOR'S ACKNOWLEDGMENTS

I HAVE RECEIVED the fullest co-operation of Mr. James K. P. Miller II, namesake and grandson of the diary's author, as well as of Mr. Arthur C. Miller, another grandson. The Miller family papers were kept safe and intact for more than fifty years by their father, Arthur J. Miller. His widow, Mrs. Helen C. Miller, has graciously supplied both encouragement and essential information to me. The Miller family made possible the editing of the original manuscript at the Henry E. Huntington Library by transferring it there for a time from the Bancroft Library of the University of California, where the original manuscript remains. Funds were provided for its editing by the Montana Historical Society, whose director, K. Ross Toole, a friend since graduate-school days, first suggested the project to me. Mr. Toole has been of material aid in encouraging its publication at every stage, from research to final printing. For this reason the book is dedicated to him. The librarian of the Montana Historical Society at Helena, Miss Virginia Walton, and her staff, have also been of genuine aid. I likewise received help from the John Randolph and Dora Haynes Foundation through Occidental College. To Professor Leonard Arrington of Utah State University goes my acknowledgment of his assistance in connection with the Salt Lake City portion of Miller's diary. And, finally, I express appreciation to my wife, Frances, and our fine sons for their companionship during two summers of traveling the "Miller trail" through Wyoming, Colorado, Utah, and Montana.

Andrew Rolle

Los Angeles, California
January 16, 1960

EDITOR'S INTRODUCTION

DESPITE THE VAST amount of literature written about the American West, diaries are still the best keys to an understanding of the vitality of life on the frontier. While multitudes of emigrants who crossed the plains kept journals and diaries, many simply wrote routine accounts concerning the length of each day's journey, hardships endured en route, and the travails of camp life for the uninitiated. Few diarists from the East grasped the flavor of the wilderness through which they passed and the sense of history inherent in the peopling of the West. Few had the ability to translate even dramatic personal experiences into accounts of lasting literary value. Most travelers were too exhausted by the demands of the trail to make more than perfunctory daily entries in the little leather-bound books in which they jotted down their accounts. Once they reached their destination, such folk found the task of adjustment to the frontier environment so absorbing that they simply abandoned their narratives.

It is, therefore, a special satisfaction when one discovers a travel account that unconsciously lights up the landscape which it describes, both on the trail and after arrival. The diary of James Knox Polk Miller is such a manuscript. Its neatly written pages were the handiwork of a young nineteen-year-old who traveled out west in the years 1864–67. Miller was born at Port Jackson, New York, on April 26, 1845. He and his sisters were orphaned early in life. Although his childhood record is sketchy, Miller, when still in his teens, went into business with an uncle at Clyde, New York. He had a disagreement with this guardian and decided to run away from home after appropriating part of the assets of his business and leaving behind a considerable debt. For this reason he adopted the pseudonym J. Sidney Osborn, an alias under which he traveled until 1875, when he revealed his true identity in a letter to a New York newspaper.

Probably his sobriquet was inspired by Thackeray's *Vanity Fair;* like his namesake in that book, Miller also possessed the capacity to experience difficulties of every sort.

Miller's trip took him to Salt Lake City and beyond. While many travelers passed through that Mormon capital in the 1860's, most did not go northward to the more remote mining camp of Virginia City, Montana, and diaries of life there during its first few years are extremely rare. Indeed, this rarity is what adds much significance to Miller's account.

After a stay of almost three years in the West, Miller left Montana for Europe in 1867. The portion of his diary printed in this book ends as he is about to sail from New York. After a trip which took him to Paris, Rome, Alexandria, Cairo, and Jerusalem, Miller returned to Helena a year, to the day, after he had left. By that time Virginia City's mines had begun to languish, and he commenced a business at Deer Lodge, buying out the mercantile establishment of William Andrews Clark, before Clark moved to Butte to become one of the copper kings of the West. Eventually Miller resumed the use of his real name and married Ada Elizabeth Miller, a cousin whom he had known in the East, and, about 1876, they moved to Deadwood, South Dakota. After his first wife died, Miller married Mary Chumasero Pope, one of the daughters of Judge William Chumasero of early Montana fame. Miller established a highly successful business at Deadwood and became one of the most important pioneer builders of that supply center for the Black Hills Gold Rush of the late 1870's. He was not only an important developer of real estate but also the president of the Deadwood Central Railroad Company, a short road to Lead, near the famous Homestake Mine. At the peak of his success Miller contracted tuberculosis and died on January 13, 1891, in Santa Barbara, California, at the age of only forty-six.

Miller's first diary starts in Chicago, where he went by railroad in the closing years of the Civil War. From that city he traveled to the river town of St. Joseph, Missouri. Miller, an unusually literate and intelligent young man, was an omnivorous reader who knew the writings of Dickens and most of the popular authors of his generation. He carried along with his diary a veritable traveling library of books.

The trails from St. Joseph, or Independence, or Westport, on the Missouri, converged upon Fort Kearny, lodestone of the Platte River country. From there Miller and various companions threaded their lonely way toward the continental divide near South Pass. He ultimately broke with the party and reached the safety of the Mormon settlements in Bear River Valley after weeks of exhausting travel through the dust and heat of the Overland Trail.

That route and the makeshift trails of the West were reasonably well plotted by the late sixties. The traveler now encountered more persons heading west than he would have ten or fifteen years before. But the hazards to life were still many. Plaguing the inexperienced were frequent Indian attacks upon overland parties, banditry on the trail as well as in the isolated new towns of the West, the risk of drowning whenever a deep, swift stream was crossed, the inevitable privations of exhaustion, and exposure to such diseases as cholera, or typhoid, and Rocky Mountain spotted fever, for which there yet existed little medical care. The animals upon which each party relied still had to find water and forage daily. By 1864–65, however, long stretches of the prairie, especially in Kansas and Nebraska, were broken by an occasional farmhouse. Farther westward—in that "mining west" of unmapped desert, mountains, and windswept rocky canyons—conditions grew more uncertain.

During his long trek Miller was especially worried about the Indian menace. Many tribes, confused by the fighting of the Civil War, which pushed Indians off their ancestral lands, vented their anger upon overland parties. From time to time, Miller saw the mutilated bodies of whites along the trail, and he dreaded standing solitary guard duty each night to prevent Indians from driving off mules and oxen.

Miller often wrote his diary entries during these evening periods. He was an eastern city boy who produced his daily account in brown ink and in a neat and careful hand. Quite understandably, his unfamiliarity with certain terms used in the West led him to misspell such words as *lariat, prairie, pony, mosquitoes, wagon, diarrhea, coyote, canyon, guerrillas, corral, bullet,* and *horizon.*

Whenever he was seized by spells of loneliness, which occurred frequently, he turned either to reading or to his diary, which he called his "only friend." On one occasion he confessed that he felt like "a few hours of quiet crying." There is a dolefulness about entries describing how the boy sat by the glow of the campfire listening to some prairie minstrels sing the "Midnight Queen." In addition to his heartaches Miller experienced the disagreements frequent among parties heading westward. His sense of independence, however, was bolstered by possession of about $3,500 in cash when he "left the states" for the West, and this sizable sum assured him a mobility denied other, less fortunate travelers.

During his three years out west young Miller managed to find himself in a variety of exciting places. In Mormon Utah he encountered an isolated, tightly organized, theocratic society whose control was increasingly threatened by the growing population of "Gentile" miners, freighters, and businessmen. In Montana, Miller found a frontier society still struggling with problems of law and order and with the difficulties of supplying an unstable population before the coming of railroads. Miller wrote of conditions as he saw them. His are not retouched recollections viewed sentimentally through the mist of time in the afterglow of old age but day-by-day diary entries. Their truthfulness, and sometimes even naïveté, comes through most vividly. Whether he described Mormons in the Great Salt Lake Basin or vigilantes in Montana, Miller was young and enthusiastic enough to savor everything he observed.

His assessment of such controversial frontier personalities as Brigham Young, Heber C. Kimball, and William A. Hickman means more when read with the simple context of such a diary than does the polemical literature written for or against either Mormons or vigilantes by persons with an axe to grind. The colorful oratory of Elder Kimball, a powerful figure in the church hierarchy, simply does not come alive in the standard printed versions of his sermons that one can consult today. The passion, verve, and even vulgarity of his style of frontier preaching could be lost to posterity were it not for an account like Miller's. Other travelers attended Mormon ceremonies at the Salt Lake Tabernacle, but few observers have so well caught the flavor of one of Mormonia's most eccentric personalities. Miller mentions even Kimball's almost unprintable asides and personal mannerisms of speaking. It is remarkable that a lad Miller's age possessed patience enough to record in detail the speeches of such church officials. His writings not only illuminate the type of oratory used in frontier Utah; they also show us what Mormonism meant to a "Gentile."

As regards Hickman, an enigmatic figure in Mormon history, Miller gives us a new view of this black-sheep lieutenant of Brigham Young who has long been called his leading hatchet man. Hickman's personality emerges as more moderate and believable than the lurid characterization published in the autobiographical *Brigham's Destroying Angel* (Salt Lake City, 1872, 1904). Although that popular work was subtitled *The Life, Confession, and Startling Disclosures of the Notorious Bill Hickman, the Danite Chief of Utah, Written by Himself,* Hickman's account of vengeance was in considerable measure the work of its editor, J. H. Beadle. Beadle portrayed a sensational Hickman, a murdering agent who efficiently disposed of unfriendly "Gentiles" and disobedient Mormons for Brigham Young. Miller, who met Hickman long before *Brigham's Destroying Angel* was printed, pictures him rather in the role of a policeman pursuing horse thieves than as a zealot who acted out of religious motives. While he exhibited wide-eyed amazement over Hickman's claim of having killed sixteen Indians in one day, he saw in that Mormon scout a person whose motivation was the protection of law and order in Utah. Diaries that help clear up such misconceptions are of great value, for myths become imbedded in history and remain unquestioned until such fresh accounts are uncovered.

Obviously under pressure to leave Salt Lake City, Miller went to Montana in disgust after a half-year's stay had reduced his savings materially. Indeed, he had to sell his coin collection of a thousand "coppers" before leaving town.

The Miller diary and other western diaries of its type challenge the conventional view of life beyond the Rockies during the Civil War. The Virginia City toward which Miller traveled after leaving the Great Basin emerges not only as the hell-roaring camp depicted by popular writers. As he struggled toward that mining hub, with his legs so swollen and raw that he wrapped part of a pillow around his feet to avoid bleeding, Miller was heading toward a metropolis which was, for him, not primarily the hurdy-gurdy town that we picture today but the center of a more stable society than is commonly attributed to Virginia City. The descriptions of Alder Gulch (and, for that matter, other such mining communities) left us by Thomas J. Dimsdale's *The Vigilantes of Montana* and Nathaniel P. Langford's *Vigilante Days and Ways* tend to overemphasize the aspect of violence. Yet these two unique books have remained almost unchallenged. Early Virginia City diaries are exceedingly rare, and the only other leading unpublished source still extant (that of James Henry Morley) is a prosaic account of day-to-day activities. Persons interested in early Virginia City thus have had to rely upon Dimsdale or Langford, and both have gone through several editions. The Miller diary provides a corrective account of substance.

The writer frequently refers to his participation in plays, sleigh rides, French and art lessons, church functions, and literary activities. Virginia City supported a theater, several bookstores, and a good frontier newspaper, the *Montana Post*.

Miller not only became a member of a lively literary society composed predominantly of men who thirsted after culture; he also joined several social groups, continued his heavy reading program, and frequently attended theatrical performances and concerts, some admittedly poor in quality. It was wholly natural that a young man like Miller, on so distant a frontier, should also participate in occasional drinking, gambling, and some pursuit of the opposite sex. The Amphion Serenaders, a group of young hellions who kept the citizenry awake nights, provided this sort of outlet. Miller experienced difficulty keeping the many good resolutions which he made. The real importance of his diary, however, lies in its modified view of the society of the West, a view generally described in Louis B. Wright's recent *Culture on the Moving Frontier*. Amid the violence, lawlessness, and crime, social, religious, and economic institutions also flourished. And Young Miller's life was influenced fully as much by merchants, bankers, farmers, artisans, educators, musicians, and artists as by vigilantes and frontier outlaws.

In some respects Miller was himself an unusual lad; in others he was almost wholly normal. He possessed the self-righteousness and moral values of many an American boy of the mid nineteenth century. He wrote of wanting himself likened to certain characters in the novel *Jane Eyre,* "at least the characters with perfect correctness." Whenever he experienced occasional fallings from grace, he was genuinely sorry. He vowed to stay away from the temptations found in saloons, billiard halls, and other murky environs toward which loneliness sometimes drove him. After visiting such spots, he would frequently acknowledge on the next day the effects of the night before, as he wrote "illness" or "sickness" into the record.

While out west, Miller tried to save as much money as possible. He wanted to travel abroad and yearned to receive a college education. He even sent for the Princeton University catalog, carefully noting the amount charged for tuition. Above all else, Miller was anxious to demonstrate his success to friends back home. Early in the diary, he made a boyish resolve never to communicate with close acquaintances or his family until he made himself rich. He also determined "to see all the world in ten years" and "never to do a dishonest action." On the latter score he boasted, on November 24, 1865, that he had "not done a single dishonest act since August 10, 1864."

One gains the impression from reading Miller's diary that he was swindled by a number of persons who took advantage of his youth and general inexperience. He possessed both unusual shrewdness in business matters and the normal credulity of youth. He could, however, be perfectly frank concerning persons who took advantage of him. About the firm of Hadley and Miner of Salt Lake City he wrote: "They owe me $180, which is probably as near as they will ever get to paying it to me."

The diary almost ignores the Civil War, which was being fought at the time it was written. He mentions the surrender of Charleston to Union forces and the occasional capture of Confederate guerrillas in Kansas and Missouri, but little other news of the war. In the isolated West, men generally were separated from the full impact of the war. Miller's political astuteness, however, was considerable, and his awareness of such a national personality as Lincoln is evident from an entry which discusses his inauguration.

Civil War Virginia City attracted more than a few draft dodgers and other ne'er-do-wells. Along with its lawyers, editors, and ministers were dance hall girls, faro dealers, and saloon keepers. Without question, Virginia City was still a wild town with some men who were quick with their guns. Montana Territory came into existence only in May, 1864, and the lawlessness of the frontier had not yet been stamped out. While Henry Plummer's notorious gang of outlaws had been uprooted by the equally ruthless vigilanteism of an indignant and aroused citizenry, plenty of thieving, whoring, and brawling still went on in the eight billiard halls, five gambling parlors, three hurdy-gurdies, and unnumbered bawdy houses and saloons along Alder Gulch.

Even during the height of the rush, however, Montanans were engaged in building the first permanent settlements in the northern Rocky Mountain country. Soon Virginia City, as well as Bannack and Helena, would be transformed from makeshift tent camps into stable communities. Miller was fortunate to find employment there with J. S. Rockfellow, one of the founders of the town who had played a prominent part in vigilante activities the year before Miller's arrival. Thus, the young man came to occupy a position of trust under one of the community's leading citizens.

By mid-1867 Miller had recouped the money lost in Utah, and he decided to head for Europe. His adventures en route to Washington and New York form one of the most interesting parts of his diary. Carrying $7,000 in gold dust for deposit in the East, Miller traveled by Wells Fargo stage from Helena to Fort Benton, the last port of call for the Missouri River steamboats. He leaves his readers a whimsical picture of an eager young man, seated alongside the hard-bitten, callow driver of this stage, talking until the "very early hours" as they rattled toward the outside world. This portion of his travels made an indelible impression upon Miller and his annoyed fellow passengers who had to push the stagecoach out of every miserable mudhole in which it became mired. Whenever the horses got stuck on the stream bottoms, the passengers were forced to walk through miles of mud, up hill and down, as the driver scowled with evident delight. Miller was relieved to reach Fort Benton, where—to the end a bookish person—he spent his time reading while waiting for his steamboat.

Once aboard the *Waverly*, the vessel that would transport him eastward, he took a boy's delight in the excitement that followed. On one occasion, after hearing a shrill whistle while he was below, he rushed up on deck, amazed to find the crew lined up along the rail shooting at a buffalo herd near the water's edge. On other occasions the steamboat stopped to trade with Indians along the riverbank.

Miller also provides us with picturesque descriptions of racing on the Missouri, a sport which few captains could resist in the golden age of steam on the western waters. Sometimes the results were catastrophic, as steamers blew up, maiming the passengers and strewing the surface of the water with wreckage. Miller's vessel on this very trip was temporarily disabled through the smashing of a paddle wheel during a race. On another occasion the *Waverly* demolished the cookhouse of a competing steamer, scattering potatoes, meat, and bread all over the surface of the river, to the delight of young Miller.

The diary indicates that a surprisingly large number of steamers were then paddling their way up and down the "Big Muddy." The *Waverly* passed forty-seven other vessels from Fort Benton to Yankton alone. At Omaha, Miller and several crew members made the mistake of overstaying their leave ashore. Then began a wild, hectic goose chase by steamer and train across eastern Kansas and northern Missouri in pursuit of the *Waverly*. Days later Miller finally arrived at St. Louis one hour before his steamer docked. He was greatly relieved to find the gold with which he had been entrusted still on board the *Waverly*. Eventually Miller reached his native East Coast and from there went on to Europe, thus temporarily ending an adventurous three years in the West.

The portion of the diary which he wrote during his western travels has been divided into four separate sections: "Chicago to Salt Lake City," "Salt Lake City and Virginia City," "Montana Territory," and "Fort Benton to Washington and New York." I have preserved the original text whenever possible, changing spelling or punctuation only where clarity could be materially enhanced. In every case such alterations are minor. I have made all date lines uniform, filled out certain abbreviations, and inserted words only where they were inadvertently omitted. Basically the diary remains as written.

THE ROAD TO VIRGINIA CITY

CHICAGO TO SALT LAKE CITY

AUGUST 10, 1864

Arrived at Chicago at 11 o'clock A.M. Cars were crowded and two hours late.

AUGUST 11, 1864

Up at 5 o'clock. After breakfast hired a livery horse and carriage & spent four hours riding about the city. Viewed Camp Douglass (from the observatory) where some six or seven thousand soldiers are confined. Rebels. Had a beautiful drive along Madison Ave., alongside of the lake. Thermometer 100° in shade. Drove across creek & through the cemetery where, tempted by the sight of the lake waves breaking up on the shore, I undertook to drive through a sandy road. My horse giving out, I was obliged to bring my ride to a close. After dinner I spent

3

the time untill seven in packing my trunk and at about 10 o'clock to sleeping on the Chicago, Burlington & Quincy R.R.

AUGUST 12, 1864

Was ousted from my very comfortable position at 5 A.M. The car I was in going to Burlington. Had a good view during the day of the immense cornfields and prairies of Illinois. At Macon City[1] we crossed an extension bridge erected in place of one burned down by . . . three weeks ago . . . from a dozzen to two dozzen armed soldiers, all carrying from one to two pistols could be seen. The R.R. folks did not provide any breakfast, acting as if it were a matter too small to be thought of. Arriving at Quincy crossed ferry connecting with H. & St. J. R.R.[2] for St. Joe. We arrived at about 11 o'clock very tired very sleepy and very glad that I had arrived at last. Riding across the large rolling prairies we had a fine view of the most glorious sunset I ever saw, four beautifull colors being in view at one time. Scarlet, purple, yellow & blue, each of the most beautifull variety of shades. Formed the acquaintance of two men bound for Salt Lake & received invitations from them to form one of a party to purchase a team & waggon, buy our own provisions, and cross the plains to S. L. City.

AUGUST 13, 1864

Up at six o'clock, descending to the "Lower Regions" of the Patee House.[3] I took $1.30 of shampooing & bathing after which proceeded to a slightly less than tolerable breakfast and then started for the center of the city, the Patee House being situated on the outskirts of the city upon an elevated piece of ground overlooking the entire city. Dust three inches thick by actual

1 Probably Macomb City, a stop on the Burlington Railroad system. See Richard C. Overton, *Burlington West* (Cambridge, Mass., 1941), 190.

2 Hannibal & St. Joseph Railroad, portions of which were built as early as 1853 to connect the Mississippi and Missouri rivers.

3 This hostelry was then one of the finest hotels in the United States. See *Daily News' History of Buchanan County and St. Joseph, Mo.* (St. Joseph, c. 1900), 295.

measurement. Met my two friends of the day before. St. Joseph is a city of about 10,000 inhabitants slightly tainted with Secession, quite pleasantly situated upon the Missouri River, its chief business seems to be in providing mules, horses, wagons, provisions etc. for Emigrants & for the western mines etc. There are two good hotels, one of them now used as a military headquarters (Patee House) and it is a sort of military beehive. Found the sleepy baggage man had delivered my trunk to Pacific Hotel & I decided in consequence to change my quarters to the Pacific. My two friends and myself spent the day in examining some 100 head of stock, trying to select a span of horses & a saddle horse. I concluded finally to select a fine pacing horse "Frank." . . . After considerable talk my friends left me, agreeing to meet me at the Pacific at 7 o'clock and to report exactly what determination they had regarding our proposed way of traveling to the Pacific States. At about eight o'clock they arrived and to my great vexation postponed the time to eight o'clock tomorrow. Very hot and dusty. Telegraphic report last night from Atchison that owing to depredations and murders committed by the Indians thin stock at the stations had been called in & no stage would start before 10 days from today.

AUGUST 14, 1864

Up at 7 o'clock, lounged about the Hotel reading "Shoulder Straps" by Henry Morford[4] awaiting the arrival of my two friends. At about 10 o'clock they arrived and we entered into the following arrangement. They are to put in $325 towards getting up an outfit to cross the plains and I am to furnish the balance of about $425.[5] I to pay them .40¢ per lb. for my baggage over 25 lbs., that is their share of it as 325 is to 425. Found their

---

4 *Shoulder-Straps, a Novel of New York and the Army* (Philadelphia, 1863), was a popular story about the Civil War, one of many similar books by this prolific author. Bound in purple cloth, it was among the volumes which Miller brought west with him.

5 It was standard procedure for western parties to go to towns near the Missouri River like St. Joseph, Independence, or Council Bluffs to be outfitted for the journey by wagon, caravan, or pack train across the plains.

names to be Geo. W. Brown & Edward Rushlow & from Rochester, N. Y. Upon concluding an arrangement we purchased a span of Bay horses for $400, Harness $35, and I purchased a fine saddle horse as before concluded, $200, looked at some wagons, made some purchases & returning to the Hotel. After supper I strolled to the river bank and returning to the Hotel retired after perusing "Shoulder Straps" awhile.

AUGUST 15, 1864

Was taken very sick during the night. Vomited very freely & had a very bad attack of Diahearea. At same time suffered a great deal of pain and did not get a moment's sleep. In morning was unable to leave my bed. Brown came up about eight o'clock, gave him $200 to purchase my saddle horse & $120 to pay on horses, he afterwards returning $10. Got down stairs about 10 o'clock very weak and without appetite, eating neither breakfast or dinner. In afternoon went to gun store & purchased three Wesson rifles, a Bowie knife, & 1000 Cartridges, I buying two of the Rifles and Rushlow one. Had to obtain Permit from the Provost before we could buy the Rifles. Obtained permit without trouble, the man belonging or having once lived at Albany. Purchased $139 worth of groceries, provisions etc., & gave $35 for wagon cover, cook stove etc. Loaded provisions into wagon so as to get an early start on the morrow. Returned to the Hotel, ate a piece of toast & drank a cup of tea after which 4 games of Billiards and I retired to Room No. 20.

AUGUST 16, 1864

Up at 5½ o'clock. Dreary drizzly rain. Purchased a dog for $3 & various merchandise needed in our trip after getting all of which, including the dog, into the wagon paid my hotel bill, a very moderate one of $9. We proceeded to the ferry crossing the Missouri River nearly rolling into the river, owing to the steep bank upon which twenty four hours of steady rain had put a coat of mud about a foot thick which, affording a very precarious footing for the horses, made crossing with a load as heavy as ours very disagreeable. It was now raining quite freely. Brown in anything but a Dry humor preferring to ride horseback to riding in our "calaboose" succeeded in getting quite damp, especially his "nether" garments, his body being protected only by an oil cloth blanket. Traveled through a fine country, fields and woods having their best dress on owing to the rain. Arriving at Walthena[6] a small town the chief points of interest being the well where we procured water for our horses, and a grocery store where we purchased a faucet for our Molasses Keg. I here mounted my pacer, the rain having ceased, & rode untill nightfall when we selected a roadside spot for our encampment covered with bushes three to four feet high & slightly sloping. Unhitching our team and riding them to water 200 yds. distant rode for the first time with only the Halter to guide by. Passing the halter through his mouth so as to form a bit it made an excellent bridle. After watering our horses we proceeded to a clump of trees a short distance off, & selecting a walnut stump, chipped off enough wood with our axe to last us, and taking our camp stove (made of sheet iron) we started a fire, Making some coffee to which of necessity we could not add milk though we carried best quality lump sugar. Cutting some dried beef & adding some hard tack we had supper after which we cleaned the horses, tied them to lairiets & divided ourselves into watches, mine being from 2 to 4½ o'clock in the morning. I laid down upon my blankets to sleep. I found it very much impossible however. The circumstances & sensations were so new to me that I could only succeed in tiring myself out trying to sleep. The chirping of the Cricket so incessant and loud, the stomping & knawing of the horses tied to our wagon, in which upon our blankets we were trying to sleep, added to our danger from Guerellas & Indians—everyone we met reporting large bands & horrible murders & massacres only 200 miles from our Encampment, causing us to keep open our rifles—made such a new sensation that I arose

6 Walthena is one and one-half miles south of Bellemont near a bend of the Missouri River. Margaret Long, *The Oregon Trail* (Denver, 1954), 37 n., 39.

having remained awake the entire night.[7] During the day we passed a Tobacco field growing finely. Also a few stalks of hemp, the first of each I had ever seen.

AUGUST 17, 1864

Our party up at 4½ o'clock. I was called in time for breakfast having had an hour's sleep. Made our breakfast of ham, coffee, & hard tack after which we greased our wagon & started. Country very beautifull. Too many hills to be called "Rolling" Plain but resembling very much. We reached Troy,[8] the county seat of Dennison County, Kansas, a village of perhaps 200 inhabitants. Here we were again regaled with stories of the attacks of the Indians by a Pale faced specimen of humanity, a Dr[agoon] who was chiefly remarkable for having small feet & boots well blacked and being one of the Militia, the last as pr his repeated statement. Passing along our route lay through what I think to be as fine a country as any in the world. Passing immense rolling Prairies on every side reaching as far as the eye can reach, with small clumps of trees from three to four miles apart, passing small farm houses, surrounded by large fields of corn. The country seems entirely destitute of fruit, water melon being the only obtainable luxury and even Potatoes are almost unknown. After indefatigable efforts to obtain a Pie of some kind we were forced to the conclusion that they were as scarce as the Potatoes. Prairie chickens, quails, Pigeons very thick. Camped about 85 miles from St. Joe in front of a farm house. Water scarce. Hard work to get wood. Supper oyster stew (poor), beef, ham & coffee. My watch until 12 o'clock. Passed a team dur-

7 Indian raids upon white settlers and immigrants traveling westward were frequent at this time. The Kiowas, Comanches, Cheyennes, Arapahoes, and Pawnees were particularly hostile after being disturbed during the Civil War. Short on rations and confused by the fighting between Union and Confederate troops, the Indians engaged in devastating raids, sometimes butchering men, women, and children with little discrimination between friend or foe. Samuel J. Crawford, *Kansas in the Sixties* (Chicago, 1911), 245–300.

8 Troy was sixteen miles from St. Joseph. Here the party was moving across northeastern Kansas. Long, *Oregon Trail*, 37. A pony express marker is on the courthouse lawn.

ing the day. Said they had brought 7 bodies, 2 wounded men, into Seneca killed by the Indians about 100 miles from our present Camp & on our route. Were also informed that we would be stopped at Seneca & not allowed to go further.

AUGUST 18, 1864

Had very good sleep. Up at daylight, 4 o'clock, breakfasted & "rolled out." Route through same description of country as yesterday. Passed Kinnekirk where we met the Overland Stage Route here coming from Atchison. Also met the first teams we had seen en route for Denver City with heads turned toward their destination, the rest having been on the homeward track scared out by Indians. Day very bright, very cold. Camped at Stage Station about 9 miles from Kinnekirk, worked untill 11 o'clock whacking our wagon after which we had supper of scrambled eggs, ham, coffee, apple sauce & soda crackers. My watch 12 to 3. Having accustomed myself to this time, to my circumstances, I found no difficulty in sleeping soundly both before and after my watch. Very heavy dew soaking boots, stockings, and feet. Bright moonlight night. The route of Pacific R.R. is intended to pass near Kinnekirk so we were informed.[9]

AUGUST 19, 1864

Up at 4½ o'clock. Very cold breakfast. Greased wagon and started. A Guerella[10] discovered a few days since among a lot of teamsters bound for Salt Lake was shot a short distance from our encampment and buried by the roadside here. Drove thirty five miles today mostly through Prairie country. Very little cultivated. We shot at Prairie chickens every little while from the wagon with our rifles. Have not killed any yet however. Passed Grenada in the morning, a small settlement of about 60 inhabitants. Passed some government wagons loaded with arms for the militia to whip out the Indians. Passed Seneca, a village

[9] Kennekuk (sometimes Kinnekuk) was thirty-six miles from St. Joseph. Long, *Oregon Trail*, 38, 39. It was a junction on the St. Joseph road with the Fort Leavenworth military road.

[10] Probably a Confederate "Bushwhacker."

of about 500 inhabitants from which the men had gone to fight the Indians. Camped at Ash Point, a city of 10 houses.[11] Took on Goods. St. Joe to Denver 204.

AUGUST 20, 1864

Up between 4 & 5 o'clock, laid in some corn and oats. Corn $1.00 Oats .75¢. Made 28 miles today arriving at Marysville toward sunset. My watch injured so as to stop it which makes it very bad. We are forced to use the following plan of ascertaining time at night, which is not always correct. We form what may be called a moon dial using the stove pipe and ground and dividing the face into three equal parts by means of Pans and axe sticks. Marysville is the largest place between St. Joe and Denver on the road. After supper Brown and myself rode to town. En route Brown, while performing an Equestrian feat, was thrown from his horse, severely damaged. After a game of billiards we returned to our wagon and as I was first watch, spreading blankets on the ground I had a fine sleep waking occasionally to see if it was all right. I shot two Prairie chickens today from wagon with rifle.

AUGUST 21, 1864

Up at daybreak. Brown and myself rode horseback to town to make some purchases if possible. As it was not possible, the stores being closed, we returned to camp. I strapped a shot gun & rifle to my saddle & started after game. At first shot my horse left me and returned to camp. I followed him and, tiard with a walk of two or three miles, spread my blanket under shade of wagon, and had a good "Nap." After sleeping awhile started again after Prairie chickens. Getting about three miles this time my horse again left me and I arrived at Camp very tiard and hungry.[12] A few crackers & molasses having constituted my din-

11 Seneca was on Nemaha Creek. Ash Point, sometimes Hickory Point, was about ninety-five miles from St. Joseph.

12 Travelers moving west often lost their animals during the first few weeks of their journey. Mules and horses sometimes ran back to their starting places as many as half a dozen times before their new owners learned to guard them more closely.

ner. After writing a sheet of paper full to Sis, Ed arrived with a fine string of fish the proceeds of his day's labors. My religious devotions to-day consisted in inquiring the whereabouts of the village church to which answer was returned that "they did not have such things in this country." Marysville, the last place for purchases, is situated on the Vermillion river. Population 500.[13]

AUGUST 22, 1864

Brown & myself rode horseback to Rock Creek and back, 34 miles altogether. Brown "took sick" on the way. No water to drink for 14 miles. At last, unable to endure it any longer, we drank from a frog pond water that resembled dirty dish water after a great deal of using. I shot 4 Prairie chickens on my way back with my rifle. Returning to camp found that Ed had somehow got possession of a chicken of the Back Yard order but it was "very" tough and not "convertible." My first watch to-night an acquaintance of mine from the other camp, a New Yorker, kindly inquired if I would accept a flask of Drake's Bitters. Afraid that my health might be poor I made a visible sign of acceptance and, leading the way about a quarter of a mile from Camp in a field of lately mown grass, he discovered a bottle of S.T. 1860X. He explained the precautions by remarking that the camp men use all sorts of liquor quite as freely as water and subsequent experience has proved it to be a fact.

AUGUST 25, 1864

Arrived at Rock Creek. Rock Creek is a stream with running water enough in it to about fill the spout of a common size tea kettle. Found about 80 teams encamped bound for Salt Lake.[14] Two trains of Mormons loaded with merchandise. Two

13 Marysville was on the east bank of the Big Blue River. It was sometimes called Big Blue and was about 125 miles from St. Joseph. During most of the 1860's it was a major stopping point for coaches of the Overland Stage Line. A few miles below Marysville was located the famous ford on the Oregon Trail called California, Independence, or Mormon Crossing.

14 Rock Creek Station would be in present-day Nebraska about 155 miles from St. Joseph. Long, *Oregon Trail*, 40.

of the trains had been driven back from the Little Blue by the Indians. The Mormons seem to be very intelligent and very gentlemanly.

AUGUST 28, 1864

Took my horse (big Frank) and went after game about 4 miles from Rock Creek. Came upon a deserted farm house a fair specimen of the condition we have generally found houses in this neighborhood. The yard & barn filled with fine hay, about a dozen chickens picking & clucking and a house cat added to the desolate appearance of the house which was in good condition excepting that everything movable, even to the window sash, had been moved. It made rather a powerful scene.

AUGUST 29, 1864

Joined a train of 34 teams and started by cross road for the Nebraska & Laramie road thus skimming the Little Blue. Made 5 miles, dined and made 7 miles and camped. Larrietted our horses and fixed my blanket under the wagon. Brown watched till one o'clock and Ed finished the night. I was taken in the early part of the night with a severe pain in my right shoulder. After spending an hour groaning and walking the ground, rubbing it severely with whiskey, it passed me somewhat. Repeating it every two hours I was enabled to pass the night. Had also attack of billious stomach.

AUGUST 30, 1864

Crossed the Big Blue at Beatrice County.[15] Fine mostly flat prairie, scarcely any houses. Camped 28 miles from Rock Creek.

AUGUST 31, 1864

Up at daylight. Felt almost well and rode ahead of train for

15 The present-day town of Beatrice is on the banks of the Big Blue River, where there were then excellent water and timber resources. Works Progress Administration, *Nebraska: A Guide to the Cornhusker State* (New York, 1939), 147–53. The luxurious growth of trees along the Big Blue were the last hardwoods emigrants found on Miller's trip west. Timber available from there on was not suitable for the repair of wagons or other vehicles.

three hours. Rolled 7 miles and dinned. Country fine, rather hilly. Met some prairie chickens. Could not get a shot. Houses very scarce, about one to every 7 miles. Passed another deserted house and took dinner here because we were not sure of water if we proceeded. Watered ourselves and horses out of a slough filled with frogs, bugs, insects, etc. I tried my hand at an oyster stew.[16] It was, to say the least, miserable. Concluded I was not a natural born cook. About 7 miles further camped. Our horses in with the herd. First time we to stand our share of guard. There is 175 horses and mules in the train that are herded every night. 4 men are with them all the while, being relieved at 12 & 3 o'clock. Their duty is to keep them together and near the camp and in case of rain or an attack to run them into the corral. Sometimes it is very pleasant work. It gives one a new impression to see for the first time a lot of mules herded together. The songs of the herdsmen, the stamping of so many feet, so large a living mass moving constantly in all directions, and yet always together, and then the chirping of the everlasting cricket. The millions of twinkling stars that with a silver moon give that certain light which leads one so imperceptibly to meditate & retrospect, all form a part of one of the pleasantries of "the life we lead."

SEPTEMBER 1, 1864

Up at daylight. Train got started about eight o'clock, traveled through a hot country. Brown & myself killed a rattlesnake. I secured the rattles. Our dog was bitten during the "melee." Shortly after as I was riding on my horse we discovered as we supposed an Antelope. Circling around about 2 miles so as to approach unperceived, blowing my horse as sun was very hot, I perceived it to be a tree. About 7 miles from our starting place we came to a "slough." Water quite cool and free from bull

16 In an age long before refrigeration western travelers refer to the use of oysters. Oyster-canning was an established business by 1850, but not until the Civil War made it necessary to provide troops with large quantities of provisions were such delicacies canned in quantity. Edgar W. Martin, *The Standard of Living in 1860, American Consumption Levels on the Eve of the Civil War* (Chicago, 1942), 18.

froggs. Watering our horses we started on, expecting the train to follow. About a mile further we came to Salt Creek where, after tying Nick the dog for fear he would poison the water, we dinned & I had a delicious bath. After washed my shirt & stockings and put them on our "clothes dryer," the bushes, and in a few moments, owing to a scortching sun, they were dry. While we were packing for a start three men came along and, entering into a conversation, we found them quite friendly and arranged to exchange some dried beef with them for Potatoes, Onions, Butter and Eggs. Accordingly we proceeded to a fine farm house and received 3 pound butter, 2 Doz. Eggs, a peck of Beans & a peck of Potatoes. Brown & myself also received all the Bread and milk we could eat and it was splendid. An old man & wife, 5 boys (tall men), & a daughter lived here . . . they were very hospitable. As a general thing the farmers in this country have neither the ability nor the inclination to furnish any food or provision other than a drink of water. Salt Creek is 35 miles from Rock Creek & 139 miles from St. Joe. Traveling 7 miles further in the hottest sun I ever saw, we camped in a valley near a slough (slo). Water very poor. Had to make some Egg Nogg with our whiskey. Larrietted our horses and fixing my blanket on the ground I fought Moskeitoes untill 2 A.M. when the weather, growing colder, they departed and I slept. Moskeitoes very ravenous biting through thick duck trousers and heavy shirt.

SEPTEMBER 2, 1864

Started late. Tried to kill some froggs but did not succeed. Killed a prairie chicken yesterday as also did Brown. Ate one last night and breakfasted on the other. Man with load of hides from Fort Kearney passed us. Reports roads clear & no Indians. Traveled 13 miles and reached the Big Blue. Crossed on a bridge, found a tolerable spring and two houses. Waited for the mule trains about two hours which we had seen leaving Salt Creek and they, not coming, we held a council of war and concluded to push ahead if not meeting any trains to Fort Kearney. Travelled to Walnut Creek. Weather intensely hot, not a drop of water on the way. Arrived about 10 o'clock at night and had considerable difficulty in finding grass and water.

SEPTEMBER 3, 1864

Up at daybreak. Busy with wagon untill 10 o'clock. Train coming up, concluded to wait untill they started. I killed with rifle, from wagon, last night two Prairie chickens, had them for breakfast. Dog [al]most well from bite of rattlesnake. Reached Beaver Creek 8 miles from Walnut Creek. Rode with a teamster, a young fellow from Hartford, Ct. Found he was escaping the law. Arriving in camp we had just time to make our night arrangements when a magnificent thunder shower arose. It was a beautifull spectacle. During the afternoon the clouds hung in heavy black masses over fully one half the heavens, occasionally showing a spot of crimson greatly resembling some infernal region of fire and flame. A low rumbling thunder was heard occasionally. Soon the clouds thickened and with the going down of the sun the storm commenced. Flashes of lightning, before only at long intervals, increased in number and beauty until the heavens presented an almost continual spectacle of most magnificent fireworks. Flash followed flash incessantly and at times the entire heavens seemed to be covered with a network of chain lightning most beautifull to behold. The edge of the Horrizon became of the most beautifull and brilliant red crimson & purple colors, looking as if on fire. Soon the Black heavy clouds covered all up. The lightning was no longer of the "chain" order. The thunder grew less frequent and soon the Heavens opened and the earth, such as was not under "cover," was deluged. When we had formed our Correl, a half mile from a ranch I jumped upon my Frank and riding to the ranch procured a watermelon and returned to camp. It being dark I could not get my horse to water. Made three beds in wagon which forced the matter somewhat as the space was small. Found lots of wild plums at our dining camp.

SEPTEMBER 4, 1864

Up early. Damp weather. Roads bad, made 18 miles & camped near Beaver Creek. Carried water about half a mile. Slept on ground. Ate very freely of some griddle cakes Ed made and they being very heavy suffered very much during the night.

SEPTEMBER 5, 1864

Started early, very cold, and very chilling wind. Rode about 14 miles horseback. Dressed in linnen pants. It commencing to rain I took refuge in wagon. Dinned at 17 mile Point on Beaver Creek 17 miles from last camp and 259 miles from St. Joe.[17] Had cold dinner. Potatoes, Ham, Soda Crackers, Molasses, and dried apples. Camped at head of Beaver Creek.

SEPTEMBER 6, 1864

Rolled 7 miles and camped at mail station house and barn, very bad order & about half used up. Our boys in team added their efforts and abstracted about a dozzen rafters in fire wood. Chased an Antelope. Went "at speed" but could not come up. Succeeded in blowing horse. Carried water over a mile from a slough. Very poor at that. Lay here all day. Stage passed us and advised us to return the rafters as they belonged to the "Overland." Terrible storm at night required all the exertions of Brown, Ed and myself to keep the wagon from being flooded with water and the covering from being blown away by the wind. Worked with might and main for an hour holding oil cloth blanket over front of wagon. Brown was soaked completely. After an hour's duration the wind died away and by dint of great exertions, in piling merchandise against the oil cloth [succeeded in] securing a little rest. Horses and mules were correlled. Very difficult to keep them in.

17 Beaver Creek runs into the Big Blue River, a tributary of the Kansas flowing southwestward. At Beaver Crossing, Seward County, Nebraska, the Overland Trail from Fort Leavenworth joined the Platte River Trail. *A History of the Origin of the Place Names Connected With the Chicago & Northwestern and Chicago, St. Paul, Minneapolis & Omaha Railways* (Chicago, 1908), 42.

SEPTEMBER 7, 1864

Drove to the Platte River about 18 miles & camped for dinner directly opposite the eastern end of Grand Island.[18] The ground and scenery here is entirely different from that we have passed heretofore. The soil is very sandy. The grass along the river is very long, almost reaching to a man's shoulders. Grand Island here is well wooded. The water from the river tastes very fine after our experience for the past few days among the "Sloughs." It is very clear. River is very low. Weather warm & pleasant. Passed large train from Virginia City. Antelopes very plenty but shy. No Prairie chickens. Made about 4 miles further and camped. Brought water nearly a mile to cook with. Stood guard over the mules with a young fellow, the Hartford man, till 12 o'clock. Moonlight night.

SEPTEMBER 8, 1864

Made 12 miles along the Platte and camped for dinner. Met great many ranch men leaving their ranches on a/c of the Indians.[19] Passed the house where the Indians made an attack three weeks ago. Three men wounded were inside. Purchased ½ bushell Potatoes, $1.50. Bag, 30¢. Indians seen yesterday 3 miles from our dinning place. Camped near the juncture of the Atchison Road. Ranches deserted all along. Brown sick, sort of cholic. Camped on the Platte. Weather fine. Moonlight untill 11 o'clock. Left Eye much inflamed One of the team shot an Antelope. Had a piece given us. Good but not very tender.

[18] Grand Island, today located north of the Platte River, is spread out upon a gradual slope rising out of the valley's broad bottom lands. It is a good example of a community determined by its position first on the Overland Trail, later on the Union Pacific Railroad, which came to the town in 1866, two years after Miller passed through. Near-by Fort Independence was completed in 1864 to combat the growing hostility of the Indians.

[19] Indian depredations reached a high point in 1864-65. Thieving bands of Sioux, Cheyennes, and Pawnees robbed overland emigrants all along the Platte River in Nebraska. Although such victims were often unhurt, emigrant parties had to be vigilant in guarding their stock, especially at night. As Miller indicates, persons who had taken up agricultural lands along the Platte abandoned them.

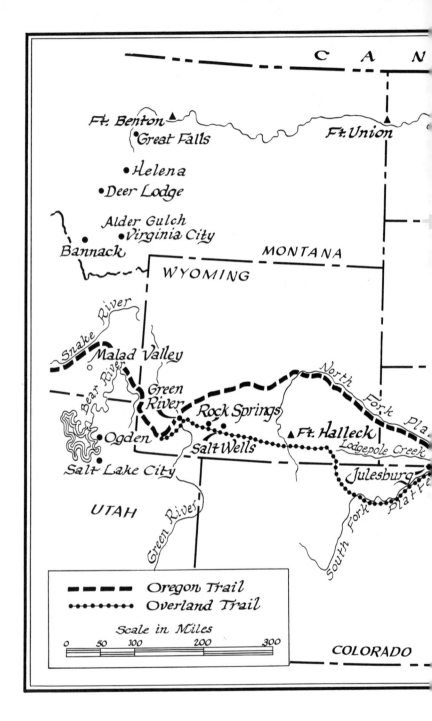

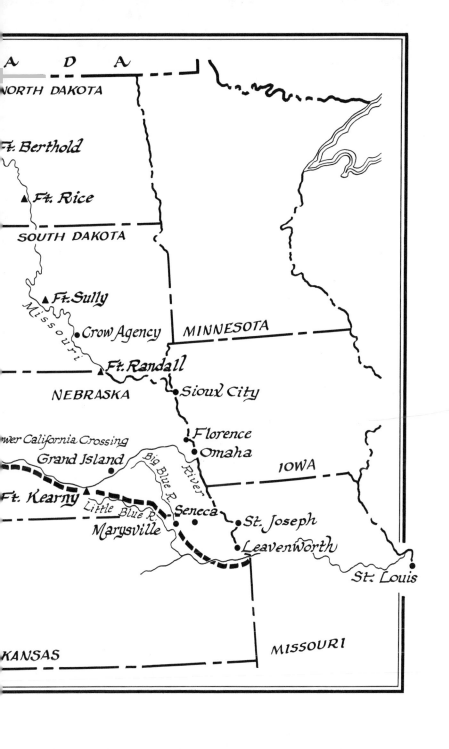

SEPTEMBER 9, 1864

Up at sunrise. Eye very bad. As was riding, reading in wagon, two Buffalo crossed the road immediately in front of us. Chased them Horseback about 3 miles. Horse at top of his speed could not get nearer than six or seven hundred yards. Very exhilerating. Lost my revolver in the chase. Reached Valley City, Fort Kearney & Kearney City. Ft. Kearney is a collection of houses & stables, about ½ dozzen wood houses the balance built of sods cut about a foot square & piled same as brick. Inside they are plastered very rough. The doors and sills are of wood. The roof sometimes is made of poles for rafters covered with sod, sometimes covered with hay, sticks & stones and sometimes the house is used for a foundation for a hay stack and covered with the hay to depth of 10, 20 & 50 feet. Kearney City is a collection of perhaps 20 houses 2 miles west of Ft. Kearney and contains perhaps 150 people.[20] Bot some tobacco of Pifer & Co. 50¢. Bought also syrup $3. Camped 5 miles west of Kearney City. Moskuitoes almost unendurable. Could not get a moment's rest during the entire night and in morning had a swollen lumped face to testify to their ferocity and power. Antelopes very numerous and tame.

SEPTEMBER 10, 1864

Camped about 25 miles beyond Kearney, had to walk 2 miles back to get water for supper. Brown hired to a waggon master to drive a team of eight mules to S. L. City. Wages $50 a month & feed. The cause of his departure was a few words he had with Ed. Near our camp is house burned by Indians. A grave beside of house. Slept on ground. Cool wind, no Moskuitoes.

SEPTEMBER 11, 1864

Camped for night 35 miles from Ft. Kearney and 375 miles

[20] At this point the party was approximately 290 miles from St. Joseph. Various emigrant trails came together at Fort Kearny. The first Fort Kearny, a blockhouse on the Missouri River, was moved westward in 1848 to give greater protection to emigrants on the Oregon Trail. Miller arrived shortly before the building of the railroad. The Kearny military reservation was ten miles square and the fort possessed various frame buildings, barracks, stables, and other fortifications, some fashioned from the sod of the surrounding prairie.

from St. Joe. Passed the grave into which eleven bodies were thrown & buried, killed by Indians about three weeks ago. They were attacked by 500 Indians and all but the wagon master massacred. No names over the grave. Nought to tell who they were and only a mound and stick to tell that any one was there buried. They are upon the roadside in a mound slightly elevated and partly surrounded by a ravine.

SEPTEMBER 12, 1864

Slept under wagon on ground. Camped off of road ¼ of a mile. Platte nearly a mile wide here. A cool wind prevented the Moskuitoes from attacking us. Innumerable stars twinkled continually and away in the west occassional flashes of Prairie lightning lit up the distant horizon and showed our position on a boundless prairie. As we were hitching up this morning we discovered a couple of Buffaloes. Saddling Frank I started after them. After an exciting chase of half an hour I finished one of them, putting a ball through his heart. Very much elated. Four of us on horseback chased him among the bluffs. After tremendous exertions with a dull knife I severed a ham and, tieing it to the saddle with the halter, I after some time arrived at camp with it. It supplied our train of 16 persons with meat 3 days. The meat is much to my taste.[21]

SEPTEMBER 13, 1864

Made about 20 miles and camped about 5 miles from Cottenwoods. Passed a platform of sticks about 10 feet high and supported by 4 poles driven in the ground. Upon the platform the corpse of an Indian with bow, arrow and hatchet, knife, etc. It is form of burial practiced by the Indians here. We are now

[21] Great herds, consisting of hundreds of thousands of these animals, were once encountered by emigrants after they reached the Platte River. By the time of Miller's journey the buffalo had been greatly reduced in numbers but were still frequently used to feed overland parties. Many believed that such game should be used cautiously and not eaten when freshly killed. Sometimes these animals, frightened both by the lightning and storms of the prairie and by emigrants, would stampede, and travelers feared these stampedes as much as Indian ambushes.

in the country of the Sioux.[22] Very windy today. Quite cold in morning, warmer in the afternoons. As we reached camp one of men shot a hare. Have to drive $\frac{1}{2}$ to one mile out of road to get water & grass when we camp.

SEPTEMBER 14, 1864

Very cold & heavy dew last night. Could not keep warm & only slept part of the time. Up early, had to get breakfast as Ed was on guard. Made some coffee and fried some Buffalo meat. This with bread, butter & syrup constituted our breakfast. There are 4 trains of us traveling together just now, 3 mule & one ox train. Had strife to get the lead, our train taking it. Passed cottonwoods about 10 o'clock. This is second point only since Kearney where we have found Inhabitants, the ranches being all deserted and presenting a most gloomy appearance. There is very little wood in the country and what little there is is contained in the houses, stables & fences of the Rancheros. The trains have very little hesitation about taking a rafter off a house or barn or a rail from the fences to replenish their camp fires in the absence of the ranch men. In consequence of which the Ranches present a most woeful tumble down appearance. The soil is rather more loamy and roads in some places very hard. The structure of the land is also changing slowly as we travel. The "bluffs" from slight elevations begin to show ledges of rock & sharp peaks. We are still upon the Platte River South Fork. I have just washed a shirt and two handkerchiefs. We lay in our stock of wood here for five or six days as there is said to be none for 120 miles. Our Bill of Fare for dinner consists of bread and molasses & cold coffee. At Cottonwoods we were 436 miles from St. Joe, 95 miles from Kearney City & 155 miles from where we struck the Platte. Camped on the Platte. Shot at three ducks which were on the slough beside the encampment. Night cold, heavy dew. Slept in wagon about the fourth time since we started.

22 The Sioux often clothed their dead in buffalo robes and hoisted them up into the cottonwoods along the Platte River.

SEPTEMBER 15, 1864

Got early start. Very cold & damp. Put on under clothes & socks. Traveled about eight miles. Left the Platte and entered the Highlands. Saw some ducks but could not hit them.

SEPTEMBER 16, 1864

As we were at breakfast this morning we espied about half a mile from us at a mail station a crowd of Indians. Old muskets, rifles, shot guns & revolvers were immediately invoked and put in running order after which, unable to discover over a dozzen, and we were 55, we started on our route, forming two Quartell [?] lines, the Indians advancing at the same time. They proved to be a party of Eleven Indians of the Sioux tribe and pretended to be on a Buffalo hunt. After talking with them some time and giving them tobacco etc. and after begging what they could they left us. Myself and two others on horseback going ahead over the hills as scouts, we shortly discovered four others in a hollow among the hills. They did not come near us but crossed. We shortly came upon Bakers Ranch and a mail station, both burned last night, the smoke of which we saw at our camp. Travelled about 16 miles today and camped upon the bottom of South Platte. Large boil upon my chin very bothersome but very well.

SEPTEMBER 17, 1864

Was somewhat surprised by Ed bursting into the wagon, where I was taking my morning nap while Ed got breakfast, crying "Indians" and making frantic effort to secure gun succeeding in which he as rapidly disappeared. I was on my feet immediately and a moment sufficed to don coat, vest, hat & one Boot. The other would not go on "instanter." When I had succeeded in getting my boot on and immerged from the wagon I found the Indians, a dozzen in number, were a great ways off. A dozzen of them it seems while we were at breakfast made a dash for our mules. Our boys happened to discover them while 300 yds. off and treated them to a dose of rifle, pistol & shot guns mixed rather too warm for them and causing them to leave in a hurry, our boys continuing to fire pistols at them when 1200 yards off. As quick as possible I saddled my horse to join three or four others who had started after them as soon as possible. Hoping to get one shot at them I arrived just in time to come back with them, the Indians having safely crossed the river. Was much vexed at myself for "being behind the times." Traveled about 20 miles and camped. My guard 12 to 6.

SEPTEMBER 18, 1864

Saw daylight and a splendid sunrise. Had rather cold guard. Expected an attack from Indians. Put the mules in Correll at 3 o'clock about an hour before sunrise. Nothing unusual happened however. Built a fire of Buffalo chips & spreading my blanket before it succeeded in keeping quite comfortable while the mules were in the Correll. Made about 20 miles and encamped at old "California Crossing."[23] First ranch occupied we have seen since cottonwoods owing to an Indian wife possessed by the ranchman, in all probability removing the fear of Indians.

SEPTEMBER 19, 1864

Got started 5½ o'clock. After traveling short distance met two stages and a number of horses. Stage stock going Back to the stations. Ranches growing thick and inhabited. Bot 2 Eggs 7½¢ a piece. Camped on a bluff. Made about 23 miles. Came to the first Rocks we had gone over.

SEPTEMBER 20, 1864

Company of soldiers 50 in number passed our camp this morning. Report that 10 soldiers were killed at Cottonwoods day before yesterday by the Indians. These 50 going to Ash Hollow about 10 miles from here to whip out some 1500 Indians there. Crossed the Platte at Julesburg, a place of four or five houses and a camp of soldiers.[24] Telegraph office here. River is

23 Sometimes referred to as "Lower California Crossing" above near-by Brule, Nebraska. Miller's party was now following the southern, or Julesburg, branch of the Oregon Trail.

about half a mile wide. Quick sand bottom. Wheels sank very deep. Our horses having a span of mules from the train hitched before them baulked & after repeated attempts we had to un-hitch them and draw the wagon out with six mules. At this place Pole Creek, or more properly, Lodge Pole Creek, empties into the Platte. One of the wagons having broken axle we had to remain here during the day. Slept awhile, smoked awhile and read awhile & went three miles to bring in a horse to be shod. Collected some brush. Quarrelled with Ed, examined my photographic album & retired.

SEPTEMBER 21, 1864

Remained in camp untill noon. Julesburg is 200 miles from Ft. Kearney and 540 from St. Joe. At noon started on Pole Creek road. I drove some mules during the afternoon for a man. Made about eight miles and camped on roadside. Grass very fine. Road hard. Buffalo chips plenty.

SEPTEMBER 22, 1864

Made about 20 miles and camped on Pole Creek.

SEPTEMBER 23, 1864

Made about 23 miles. Camped on Pole Creek. Road good and country hilly.

SEPTEMBER 24, 1864

Saddled Frank and rode over the Bluffs in search of Antelopes. Saw 12 or 14 but could not get a shot. Also saw a red Fox. Country beyond the Bluffs hilly and well covered with grass. Returning to the road found our horses stuck in the sand where

[24] Julesburg is in modern Colorado. It was a pony express station from 1860–61 and was named for Jules Beni (sometimes Reni), who had a trading post at the "Upper Crossing" of the Platte before 1860. An Overland stage station, Julesburg was burned in an Indian raid on February 2, 1865, only a few months after Miller passed through it. Margaret Long, *The Smoky Hill Trail* (Denver, 1953), 172–74, Works Progress Administration, *Colorado: A Guide to the Highest State* (New York, 1941), 208–209, and Works Progress Administration, *Wyoming: A Guide to Its History, Highways, and People* (New York, 1941) 301–302.

the road crossess the creek bed. Had to borrow two mules to pull out. Traveled untill after Sundown and camped by road side on small hill. It being my guard from 12 o'clock I made a quick supper and to insure going to sleep quickly took a swallow of Old Rye & Sugar and retired to sleep in the wagon.

SEPTEMBER 25, 1864

Was called for guard at 2 o'clock. Taking my rifle I was on guard untill after breakfast. Right dark untill about 2 A.M. when the moon arose. Great number of stars visible. Drove the mules to water at day Break. This is the 3d night I have herded mules and have found neither comfort nor convenience in it. My guard every seventh night. We are now comming into high country. Prickly pears every where and often are felt when not visible. A few sage Brushes begin to be seen. Antelope very thick & very shy. Rode horseback from six to 10 o'clock over the hills after them but only succeeded in increasing my ability to sleep. Returning to wagon, not withstanding the rather uncertain stability of the wagon soon fell asleep & was awakened by Ed intruding among the composites of my bed in search of something to eat. Made about 20 miles today. Met train of wagons from Virginia City crowded with men returning, not having made their expected strikes and returning in disgust—and in want. Had to guard mules untill after supper. After taking a light supper I reclined to the Arms of Morpheus with my arms (Fire Arms) under my pillow.

SEPTEMBER 26, 1864

Was awakened by Ed calling to breakfast. Reached Pine Point about noon and all hands started after wood. We having met no wood for 120 miles before and there being 70 miles ahead we made no fires. When out of wood we used weeds, sticks, and Buffalo Chips. From the top of Pine Point can be seen the Black Hills. Traveled untill after sun down and camped just as it was growing dark. Beautifull glorious sunset.

SEPTEMBER 27, 1864

Started at about six o'clock. Traveled about 12 miles, met a French Mexican with Indian Poney & three Antelopes he had killed. Paid him $1.25 for the ham off one of them. While trying for fish I startled a large Hair [hare] about 10 feet from me. Travelled untill dark and finding no water traveled about 2 hours in the dark being hardly able to keep the road and missing it once. Frank baulked and we concluded to camp. Having no water most of them went to bed supperless. We accidently having half a cup of coffee apiece left, added crackers, apple sauce and syrup and did very well. Cold & chilly night.

SEPTEMBER 28, 1864

Started as soon as it was light and traveling about eight miles came to water. Very cold & chilly. Met a "Kiota"[25] or small wolf & shot at him at about six hundred yards and—missed. Camped on Pole Creek a stream two inches deep and as many feet wide. Grass poor. Camped on a hill slightly elevated. At about 12 o'clock A.M. we finished our breakfast & "Rolled on." After going about eight miles we camped in the road about a mile from water. About 4 o'clock A.M. another man and myself took our rifles and started after Antelope. After wasting three shots on a flock of ducks I hunted Antelopes untill after sundown & returned to camp with our game. Cold wind today untill noon. Ed let off his rifle accidentally. Brown had same experience twice. Fortunately Ed only hurt a pile of harness. Other train's gone ahead.

SEPTEMBER 29, 1864

Very cold night. Ice Frozen ¾ of an inch in water pails. Did not go to bed untill 12 o'clock, passing around the cigars. We all seated ourselves around a camp fire and yarned and smoked the time away. Camped in sight of "Black Hills" and in sight of some very white hills covered with snow—Ugh!

25 Coyote.

Camped on the ruins of Fort Wallback,[26] an Indian fort of some importance in its day. All remaining now is the chimney of the different Buildings they being of stone and indestructable. Arriving at 3 o'clock took my rifle and started over Black Hills after Antelope with three others. Had to ascend some very high hills on our route the view from which was very grand. There is here acres upon acres of excellent quality of Ochre. After hunting untill dark without getting game I returned to camp. Supped on Antelope meat, Potatoes, Onions, Bread, Syrup & coffee.

SEPTEMBER 30, 1864

Camp was "beat up" at about 3 o'clock. Drove 28 miles & camped in the Big Laramie. Our route today lay over "divide" said to be part of the Rocky Mountains. A very chilling wind kept me inside of the wagon most of the afternoon. Ed driving, made about eight miles from last camp & took in wood for 55 miles. Crossed very little level country and many hills & bluffs, our horses stalling at the largest hill. Country very rockey. A few trees, Pine, scattered over the hills. Passed two or three pine forrests, the wind whistling through which made a steady surge sounding like the steady sound of an immense flock of birds. A few sage bushes and many "mountain Bushes." Reached a Valley through which could be seen 13 miles distant the "Big Laramie."[27]

OCTOBER 1, 1864

Up at 5 o'clock. Breakfast bean soup, coffee & bread. Horses

26 A "Fort Wallback" is difficult to identify. Near present-day Merino are the remains of Fort Wicked, once a ranch and station on the Oregon Trail destroyed by the Indians. The natives involved in that raid spoke of the station-master of the Overland stage station here as "old wicked." WPA, *Colorado Guide*, 201. Fort Wallace, on the Smoky Hill River in Kansas, was built only in 1865 and could hardly have been the site mentioned by Miller. There was, however, a Camp Walbach on Lodgepole Creek in Wyoming which was used as a stopping place by emigrant parties. Agnes Wright Spring, *The Cheyenne and Black Hills Stage and Express Route* (Glendale, 1949), 109. It seems likely that Miller's route was up Lodgepole Creek from the south fork of the Platte.

27 Here the party veered northward out of Colorado into present-day Wyoming and the valley of the Laramie River. It traveled off the regular Overland Trail.

stalled in crossing Big Laramie. Water from six to 14 inches deep & "below zero." Getting excited I jumped in and "Black Snaked the horses" quite lively and succeeded in soaking boots, pants, stockings, etc. but did *not* succeed in starting team Hitching a span of mules we finally emmerged. Cold wind & cloudy. Ed proposed to take a drink of whiskey and not withstanding my declining fixed enough for both and, in my declining, drank it all. Shortly afterwards, disputing about some trifling matter, he became half crazy with anger and at one moment I made up my mind that one of us would need take a bullett before it was quieted as that is the fashionable way to settle disputes in this country. Waiting untill he had "blowed out" I informed him that he acted as if under the influence of liquor but that if he wanted to make a quarrel it must be a "serious" one as I would not descend to a fist fight. This somewhat cooled him and gave me an opportunity to talk to him and in a few moments the man was crying as if his heart would break. I told him that I would not travel with him a mile beyond the first mail station and offered him $20 to take my place to drive the wagon through. The result of this quarrel impressed me with one thing very forcefully, the superiority of a person perfectly cool and self possessed to one under the influence of passion. Not allowing a single angry word to escape me, not giving a peg though badly scared, Ed afterward tried every way imaginable to make it up. Reached Little Laramie about 3 o'clock. Cold wind and rain. Sold ½ gal. whiskey at $6 per gal. Spent the after noon in keeping myself warm. Hired Ed to stand my guard from 12 to 6 o'clock for $1.40.

OCTOBER 2, 1864

Snowed from midnight untill 10 A.M. about 2 inches deep. Water froze hard. Made 15 miles and camped at mail station. Cold chilling wind drove all day. Concluded arrangements to leave tonight by stage. Received six letters to deliver for the train boys. Took my last camp meal. Packed satchel & started for station. I gave Ed $20 & $1.50 for standing my guard once in seven days. Comfortable quarters in mail station. At about 10 o'clock stage arrived and thus ends a trip of 48 days on the Plains with a mule train, a quite pleasant one and quite new to me. Traveled about 1390 miles.

OCTOBER 3, 1864

Very cold last night, having brought no blankets and my book being yet wet. I found crossing among the mountains quite a cold job. Sleep was out of the question and I had considerable difficulty to keep my feet from freezing. Warm day. Reached Fort Halleck.[28] Thirty eight miles at 4 A.M. Good breakfast for $1.50. Purchased a ticket here for $107 to Salt Lake. Slept all day among the straw on the bottom of the stage, I being the only passenger. Dined at North Platte,[29] good dinner. Bought a Buffalo robe for $8. Drove with driver to pine point [to] find him a Buck Eye and he has traveled with Dan Rice. Supper at Sulphur Springs. During the after noon from 2 to 6 rode with driver. At six took to my "Hay" and slept till 11 o'clock when I was awakened by arrival at Sulphur Springs about 100 miles from Fort Halleck. The station keeper here has a young black bear very full of "tricks upon travellers." He did not play any upon me, however, out of respect for my age.

OCTOBER 4, 1864

Supper finished by 12 and started. Spent the remainder of the night in vainly endeavoring to sleep. Reached La Clede [at] head of Bitter Creek at two, 55 miles from Sulphur Springs where a driver got on who was acquainted with L. M. of Ohio, Sis' friend at F. He also was acquainted with Van Amburgh and gave me some valuable information regarding circuses. Rode untill 9 o'clock when I again tried to sleep. With what success

28 Fort Halleck, in present-day Wyoming, was named for Major General H. W. Halleck. It was a strategic cavalry post and station on the overland stage route. Earlier in the year of Miller's arrival a party of soldiers was caught there in one of the worst blizzards of Wyoming's history. WPA, *Wyoming Guide*, 237.

29 Miller here obviously means the North Platte River in the modern Medicine Bow National Forest rather than the town of North Platte many miles to the east, in Nebraska.

I can hardly determine with much assurance, the driver asserting that I snored tremendously. At Salt Wells 54 miles from La Clede & 209 from Halleck, where we arrived at 4 o'clock, made some cakes of flour and water. Fried some antelope meat and this, with some salt wells water, constituted our Bill of Fare. The water here is very strongly impregnated with salt, three wells having been dug before finding one fit to use. We are now across the Great Alkali Desert watered by Bitter Creek. The water is miserable and in many places can not be used, being fatal to man & beast owing to the alkali beds through which it runs. Reached Rock Springs at about 11 o'clock, 15 miles from Salt Springs. Bought a pint of whiskey for which I paid $5 and spilled ¾ of it. Weather warm. No people in Mail Stations, no plant but sage. We meet hundreds of people almost daily coming from Virginia City out of provisions, some in starving condition. Arrived at Green River where the land lady, being sick, had "pickings" for dinner. Rather rough.

OCTOBER 6, 1864

Breakfasted at 4 A.M. horrible. Good dinner at Bear River. Butter, custard, buttermilk. On this river are the Mormon settlements. We are now coming among the canons. Passed Needle Cliffs. Grass improving very rapidly & sage bushes disappearing. Bear River is 90 miles from Salt Lake City.[30] Saw first newspaper that I had seen in 51 days. Supper at head of Echo [Canyon] where resides an old eastern lady from Delaware. Passed through Echo Canyon by moonlight. It is a grand drive. At a place where in 1845 the Mormons erected fortifications the rocks overhang the road to the hight of 1500 feet.[31] A creek along which the beavers have built numerous dams is the only sonnet, save that of the stage, which disturbs the solemn majestic silence. Reached foot of Echo Canon at midnight. Very sleepy. Runaway

[30] In the extreme southwestern corner of present-day Wyoming. The valley opened up easy access toward the south and Salt Lake City itself. Overland emigrants usually welcomed arrival in this "green wilderness." Here Miller had definitely entered into the geographical orbit of Mormon influence.

[31] Actually in 1857 during the Utah War.

horses. Driver afraid. Grizzly bear seen at station 10 miles from here.

OCTOBER 7, 1864

Slept a little. Bitter cold before sunrise. Passed through a canon and breakfasted. Drove over the Little mountain road, a splendid road but somewhat dusty and reached Salt Lake at about 11 o'clock.

SALT LAKE CITY AND VIRGINIA CITY

OCTOBER 19, 1864

Saw summit of the highest mountain in Salt Lake Valley. Started at 8 o'clock this morning to ascend a mountain which I supposed was about 3 mile walk from the Salt Lake house.[1] Arrived at the "base" of the mountain at two o'clock and after exhausting labor of 3½ hours I find my self near the summit where I pen this at 5:35 P.M. I could ascend easily to the summit but as it is growing both dark and cold I think I would not risk life by remaining longer [on] Twin Peak, 11,660 ft. high.

After writing the above I commenced the descent, having about half an hour of light left. I, by dint of hard labor, succeeded in getting down the rock part of the mountain which was almost perpendicular and in reaching a ravine. I now find it impossible, on account of the darkness to guide myself in the

[1] Salt Lake House was a noted Mormon hostelry.

smallest degree by the sense of seeing and now my work began. Keeping in the bottom of the ravine as well as I could, I stumbled along over rocks into holes, often thrown down, twice turning complete somersets, expecting every moment to end up with a sprained ankle, tired and exhausted and half dead from thirst on a/c of the dust which, coating bushes etc., was transferred by my efforts to my mouth and lungs. I arrived at the foot of the mountain entirely "played out." Seeing some lights in the distance where the settlements were, I endeavored to make my way to them. I soon became entirely mixed in some half a dozen streams and ditches, some of them almost impassable with daylight and entirely so at night.[2] After wandering about for half an hour, I found myself in front of the house where I had dined which I had approached without knowing it. My thirst I had satisfied with two or three hats full of water from a ditch, and I soon satisfied my hunger with bread and milk, the best the house afforded. I also had an opportunity of examining damages and found them to consist of sundry cuts, bruizes and scratches in hands & face, sundry knocks on shins, sundry holes in boots. My coat ruined in holes and my pants litterally picked to peices, my necktie gone heavenward, that is, left on some passing bush. Happy to have escaped without being injured to the death or bed, I departed after inquiring out several places and recieving a very ungracious reply to my asking for lodgings. A "Poor" couple took pity on me or on the "double price" I offered and I was permitted to occupy a quilt on the floor with a Petticoat for covering, with a "country [hick]," an uncouth specimen of farm production who kept me awake all night. In the morning I made breakfast out of tea and molassess, peaches and molassess, molassess & eggs & bread. Walking 12 miles I arrived at the hotel at about 11 o'clock quite "played out." Reaching my room I thought the hard bed a couch most soft and luxurious. The view of the valley from the mountain top was grand, some 60 square miles lay spread out before me hemned in by mountains on three sides and by Great Salt Lake on the other and traversed by in-

2 Probably many of these obstructions were irrigation canals.

numerable ditches conveying the water over all parts of it, the stubble of different graines resembling much a chess board each being of different color and certainly a game of life was fully indicated by farm houses of all sizes and shapes and scattered over every part. In the distance Great Salt Lake City—with its square regular streets shaded with trees, its peach and apple orchards, the square occupied by President Brigham Young covering three square miles of Ground beautiful but small.

OCTOBER 26, 1864

Having been in the city long enough to determine something about them, have concluded to give my experience: "Description of Salt Lake country & People." Salt Lake City is situated at the base of a chain of mountains forming the northern limits of the city; to the east and south the Valley through which the Jordan[3] flows and to the west the Population is about 10,000, composed of about ¾ Mormons and ¼ Gentiles. The city situated upon the slope at the foot of the mountains. Part of the Sierra Nevada [actually the Wasatch Range of the Rocky Mountains] slopes gradually toward the valley making available numerous small mountain streams for city purposes such as turning machinery for manufacturing purposes. At the head of the slope nearest the mountains are situated the Buildings belonging to and used by the "President" and head of the Mormons, Brigham Young. They are formed in two large squares, in one of which is the "Tabernacle" or church and the cite of the Mormon Temple, the foundation of which is already laid. This Square or "Block" is surrounded by a wall three foot thick made of adobe bricks mounted into heavy stone caps. The other square contains the President's House, Tithing office, School house, Stables, Mach[inery] etc.[4] This Block is also surrounded by a wall made of paving stone joined and held together by a lime cement about three feet thick with heavy frame gates and doors, porters houses

3 The Jordan River flows from the fresh-water Utah Lake into Great Salt Lake.

4 By "machinery" Miller meant a blacksmith shop, a grist mill, and probably a foundry on Temple Square.

etc. The wall is in both cases about 12 feet high. About three miles northeast of the city is Camp Douglas at which point Gen. Connor's command is situated consisting of from 2 to 5 thousand men as the case may be.[5] Both guns from the fort command Brigham's house.

NOVEMBER 5, 1864

Having hired the corner of the Billiard saloon and the corner of the city Restaurent, I this day for first time run both of them. I pay $100 a month for one corner and 75 for the other, $100 for one more and 50 for another. My monthly expenses are about $385. Up till 2 o'clock. Very hard work.

DECEMBER 4, 1864

Up at 9½ o'clock. Rained and snowed about the entire night the effect of which is visable in the muddy sloppy streets. Attended to my cigar stand all day. Day before yesterday rented stand in Chad and Davis Grocery store for John Van Ness, an acquaintance of mine I knew 8 years ago. I give him the goods he wants to sell and give him all the profit he makes on goods up to $100 a month, on all over that 10%.

DECEMBER 5, 1864

Up at ½ past six. Business dull, profit $3.50 all told today. Agreed today to commence early in the spring a course of travel embracing "the world" on the cheap plan, having in view adventure and improvement. Drank a Tom and Jerry to our success. John Van Ness who is going and myself cost $1. Lost a game of billiards, another $1, reducing the day's profit on all my business to $1.50. Have my breakfast at the restaurent in the building, my dinner and supper is brought to the stand. Get 25% commission on selling books. To bed at 12 o'clock P.M.

DECEMBER 6, 1864

Up at 8 o'clock. Change in the weather. Mud which yester-

[5] This estimate of the number of troops at Camp Douglas, named after Stephen A. Douglas, is high. It is doubtful that Connor had more than 1,500 troops.

day was from one to twenty inches deep partially dried up. Sky cloudy but dry. Made $4.74 on cigars sold at auction. I do them up in bunches of 15 and by that process get 7 cents apiece, cost 5 cents. Weather warm. Gamblers drunk, fight in the Gamblers quarters down stairs. Pistols drawn, not used. Martin closed bar at 9½ o'clock and Billiard Saloon at 10 o'clock. Hurt my business. Bed 12 o'clock.

DECEMBER 7, 1864

Up at 8 o'clock. Saloon closed because of a number of gamblers being drunk and two of them going to fight a dual. Trade dull, lost $2.50 on Day's sales. "Relieved" at about 10 P.M. Rather "out."

DECEMBER 8, 1864

Up at about 8 o'clock. Reduced my expenses today to $10.34, a decrease of $1.66 per day by discharging a man and then hireing him at a lower price. Trade very dull in the eating Saloon, not paying expenses. Cleared $6.21 on days work. Johnny played at Camp Douglass last night clearing $8. Have not done a dishonest action since I left the states.[6] Ran [up] 19 points on a game of billiards. Fully determined to commence a tour of the world in the spring time. Sun shiny weather.

DECEMBER 9, 1864

Up at about 8 o'clock A.M.

DECEMBER 16, 1864

Day before yesterday at about 10 o'clock at night as I was behind my counter a gentlemanly appearing, well dressed man calling himself Grey attracted my attention by keeping a little too near my stand to suit me. Directly opposite the stand is the bar behind which is a very fine large glass. Leaning my head on my hands, I was able to watch his movements with the aid of

---

[6] A remarkably ingenuous statement that tends to encourage one to believe in Miller's truthfulness elsewhere in the diary.

the looking glass without rousing his suspicions. He was trying to steal books. I thought myself mistaken as he did not take any. When I came to "retire" I discovered myself short a Smith and Wessons Revolver worth $28. In the morning going round to the gun stores and auctions I found it had been left at an auction room and $15 received on it. Identified it.

DECEMBER 17, 1864

Rec'd my revolver again.

DECEMBER 18, 1864

Up at 9 o'clock. Good business. Sold $75, cleared $12.

DECEMBER 19, 1864

Up at 8 o'clock. Policemen arrested two men for stealing my Revolver, each denying and accusing the other of the theft, one was fined $15 and in the mean time the other had been proved to have stolen about $300 worth of Gloves and was sent to the penetentiary. Changed my boarding place to the "City Restaurant," the cause of the change, Frenchy putting sugar in my coffee after my repeated requests to him not to do so. Business tolerable. Profit $8. Denniss and a gambler playing billiards kept me up till nearly 2 A.M.

DECEMBER 20, 1864

Cold night. Slept cold and "steady by jerks," the fire at 6 o'clock being built by Dennis[s] added to my comfort and I slept till awakened by Dan's inquiring if I wanted any breakfast. Johnny Van Ness coming from camp. Spent an hour or two trying to sell some cigars around among the saloons etc. Sold 100 at $5 pr. it being good luck. Was requested to be at Court House at 4 P.M. Trial of Mr. Grey. Went. To trial tomorrow 10 o'clock A.M.

DECEMBER 23, 1864

Busy preparing for Christmas which is to be celebrated to-morrow.[?] ·

DECEMBER 24, 1864

Fair Weather. Sales in my three stands[7] $120.00 giving me profit of about $30.00.

DECEMBER 25, 1864

Up at 9 o'clock. Christmas celebrated today by numerous boys prowling about the streets yelling "Christmas gifts" in crowds of from 20 to 30, also by a *select* crowd of half a dozzen who have been drinking all day in the Billiard Saloon on a bust. Billy the barkeeper is one of the "crowd." Breakfasted at about 11 o'clock and dined at 5 o'clock on Roast Turkey, Roast Pig and Plum pie. Excepting at breakfast and dinner I spent the Bal. of the day behind my counter reading "What will he do with it" by Sir Edward Bulwer Lytton.[8] Did not use any intoxicating drinks during the day and retired early at about 11 o'clock. And thus passed the 20th Christmas it has been my very fortunate lot to hail in this "subhuman sphere."

DECEMBER 26, 1864

Up at 7½ o'clock. Christmas again to day. All stores closed. Every body trying to get drunk and their efforts meeting with very commendable success.

DECEMBER 27, 1864

Christmas "played out." Everybody late abed except Mr. Martin who is around about two hours earlier than usual prompted by a very unusual resolve to oversee cleaning the snow from the roof of the Billiard Saloon. Trade tolerable poor. Paid note of

---

[7] It is noteworthy that Miller and other "Gentiles" should be selling tobacco among a people who theoretically were not supposed to drink or smoke. He was able to sell such commodities as cigars at $5.00 apiece because Salt Lake City had already become a supply center after the discovery of mines in the early 1860's in the intermountain regions of northern Utah, western Colorado, and western Montana. The movement in and out of Salt Lake City of both miners and soldiers aided suppliers like Miller and helped make the Deseret region no longer a homogeneous, independent community of Mormons. Orthodox Mormons greeted with revulsion the scenes of drunkenness described by Miller.

[8] *What Will He Do with It? A Novel* (New York, 1859).

$150. Started a new Establishment today which makes 4 institutions that I am the lawfull owner of. Up till 1 o'clock A.M. Finished "What will he do with it," a very superior novel. Highly instructive and amusing.

DECEMBER 28, 1864

Up at 8 A.M. Johnny down from camp. Feels rather "Blue." Poor houses are the cause. The last institution seems to be rather a non-paying one, the profits on the first day being 2¢, but as that will pay the rent, commissions, and leave me 1¢, I should not complain. Renewed note today of $600 at 5% interest. Trade very dull. Profits on my four stands, $100. Running my hand through a pane of glass, thereby clearing the way for a current of wind over my bed, I have fully prepared myself for a cold. Attended theater with a young man from New York state. Play was "Belphegor the Mountebank."⁹ Pauncefort was the "star." Female acting poor, balance was passable. Brigham Young's Daughter (married) played the part of the Mountebank's son. Well performed by her. Fair looking, very fine form.¹⁰ I am now slightly homesick, a morbid affliction which always comes to me when I see others enjoying Family, relatives, and friends, sisters, mothers & sweet hearts and remember that I am alone. Well the future is before me. I am not afraid to approach it, resolving never to return to my home untill I can buy golden opinions of every former friend. I am not inclined to seek wealth just now. First I would see the World. I would study and enjoy all the different attractions which God has scattered over the earth. I would deserve the name of "traveller" and be able to return not

9 Salt Lake City *Deseret News*, December 28, 1864, reviews this "capital Christmas piece" on page 2. This play was performed at the Salt Lake Theater, constructed in 1862 by Brigham Young and the Church of Jesus Christ of Latter-day Saints (commonly called Mormon Church) at a cost of $100,000. It was modeled after the Drury Lane Theater in London and was equal in its appointments to other leading theatrical houses. See George D. Pyper, *Romance of An Old Play House* (Salt Lake City, 1928).

10 Brigham Young had several daughters who acted in the theater. He took a personal interest, attending regularly, often with his large family. Among these daughters was Mrs. Hiram Clawson, who acted in the play which Miller saw.

Pencil sketch of Mormon tabernacle in Miller's diary, April 6, 1865.

James K. P. Miller (right) and friends at Salt Lake City in 1865, just before leaving for Virginia City.

only with wealth but with an experience that will mature my judgement and will furnish to my thoughts subjects healthy, improving, and elevating, and withal, interesting. I would make first the Book solid, valuable, improving, and imperishable. I would then gild the cover and finish my work with the golden clasp of Wealth. Having bound my work with Kind Philanthropy I will have attained all which I now desire. Will I succeed or is my career to become ignoble, short, or unfortunate? God knows and time will disclose his knowledge. Retired 1 o'clock.

DECEMBER 29, 1864

Up at 8½ o'clock. Business Better. Made some purchases in view of my intended excursion in the spring at auction, a Buck skin vest for $4.00, a Beaver Vest $11.75, a pair blankets $8. Johnny down from camp. Long talk. Staid up all night. Cleared $5 on days work. Bed 1 o'clock.

DECEMBER 31, 1864

Slept late up 9 o'clock last day of 1864. Weather clear cold and frosty. Dull, Duller, Dullest. Spent New Year Eve in a Decidedly dull style.

JANUARY 1, 1865

Spent New Year about the same way that spent Christmas. Commencement of 1865. No New Years calls nor "Happy New Years." Well a stranger among strangers need not ask to be let alone. How many changes 1864 brought to me. I have lived a life in that time and seen more changes than in all the other years of my life. I start 1865 with good resolutions as follows:

> Never do a dishonest action
> Never to do a dishonerable action
> Never to get drunk
> Not to play billiards while in Great Salt Lake City
> otherwise than good or doubtfull To see all the World
> within two years.

To have no communication with my family until I am in *want* or *rich*

JANUARY 8, 1865

Up at 8 o'clock. Attended Mormon service in Tabernacle at 10 A.M. Very cold in church, very moderate sermon. Attended again at 2 P.M. Brigham Young spoke, subject: What does God look like. Disposition like Jesus, hence like any man. At 6 P.M. attended 13th Ward. Amasa Lyman, one of the twelve apostles, lectured on Preaching etc., a quite able discourse, but, as usual in the Mormon teachers, very rambling.[11] Very friendly to the Gentiles, that is he did not abuse and execrate them which is the almost universal and constant practice among them. Much disturbed by a "wooley Poodle" and large shepards dog who were determined and quite succeeded in making a commotion among the ladies.

JANUARY 11, 1865

Up at 7 o'clock. Business very dull for the last three days, just paying expenses. Sold some keep sakes today, two matts worked By and given me by Mary, and those given me by Julie. Whole brought $5. Had a long conversation and argument last evening with two rabid Mormons. Nothing could disabuse their minds that the United States before many years would belong to the Mormons and Brigham Young be President and that all the world would be at war except the Mormons within a few years.

JANUARY 15, 1865

Up at 8½ A.M. Weather very cold. John down from camp. Attended 14th Ward meeting, it was held in the 14th ward assembly rooms.[12] At the time of my entrance the choir were sing-

11 Amasa Lyman, with Charles C. Rich, was a leading figure in the settlement of the Mormons at San Bernardino, California, in the period 1851–57.

12 In Mormon Church organization the smallest unit is the ward, equivalent to a village settlement or, in the case of a large community like Salt Lake

ing. The music was very deserving of praise, the instruments being three violins, one bass viol and Melodean. The services were opened by Mr. Wilford Woodruff, a very fluent and copious Speaker and quite sufficiently versed in the scriptures, especially the old, to be able to secure all the benefit possible from those parts convertable to the benefit of Mormonism.[13] His discourse occupied considerable time and was followed by a discourse from Geo. Cu-Cannon which possessed neither the ability nor sense of Woodruff's remarks, all his remarks tending to impress upon the Mormons the idea that they are under most explicit obedience to the heads of the Church. As Mr. Cannon is private secretary to Brigham Young his remarks sounded as if they first saw light in Brigham's closet and were merely his (Brigham's) efforts to extend and increase his power.[14] The Assembly room is very finely finished, the wall in shape of cresint over head and very white, two fine chandeliers of kerosene oil lamps. A fine Moulding and cornice, Heavy damask curtains, everything combining to make it very pleasant and attractive. The audience was, taken as a whole, as fine as I ever saw in the states in a city of this size. Among them two of Brigham's daughters.

JANUARY 16, 1865

Very cold night, cold morning. Business dull. Noon, cold, cause unknown. I am homesick tonight. Have turned to my "Diary" and written the above to turn my thoughts from success. Must try something else. Would like a few hours of quiet crying if I were not sure it is very foolish. Bought a Smith and Wessons rifle today with 350 cartridges, $30.

City, to several blocks in the city. The size of a ward usually varied from 200 to a 1,000 persons. Each ward had its own meeting house with a bishop in charge.

13 Wilford Woodruff was one of the Twelve Apostles of the Mormon Church and later became president of the church from 1887 until his death in 1898. Mathias F. Cowley (ed.), *Wilford Woodruff* (Salt Lake City, 1909).

14 George Quayle Cannon at this time was not only Brigham Young's personal secretary but was considered one of the foremost orators and writers of Mormonism. He became a delegate to Congress in the 1870's and 1880's and was made a member of the powerful First Presidency of the church after the death of Brigham Young in 1877. Andrew Jenson, *Latter-day Saint Biographical Encyclopedia* (2 vols., Salt Lake City, 1901–36), I, 42–51.

43

JANUARY 30, 1865

Attended Mrs. Cook's concert commencing at 7 o'clock P.M. Tickets $1.00. Mrs. Cook assisted by her pupils Son and two or three ladies as volenteers treated the audience to "Strains of Sweet Music" until 11 o'clock concisting in very large proportion of duetts on the P. F. [pianoforte]. One of the "Girls" bore so marked a resemblance to my sister Emma that only half my time was occupied by thoughts of the exercises. Half the time I was thinking of "Home Sweet Home." Very poor house. Mrs. Cook being a poor widow woman and I feeling pity for the poor success which attended her long and laborious efforts, the prospect being that not only would she be without profits but would loose through expenses, I [passed] a $5 Treasury "Greenback" to another gentleman, Billy Sheppard, adding $5, I wrapped them in the programe and directing to Mrs. Cook with request for "Rock-Me-to-sleep-mother." Billy taking advantage of a moment of applause, threw it upon the stage. A short time after, Mrs. Cook, stepping to the front of the stage, remarked that as she had not the music for "Rock me to sleep Mother" she was of necessity unable to gratify the wish of the lady or gentleman who threw the note upon the stage, who would please accept her sincere thanks, fixing her eye on our corner as she spoke. I record this incident merely to show that I have done "the first" good deed this Bright year, 1865 and to testify to the pleasure which so well repays one for a deed of kindness and charity. Weather fine.

JANUARY 31, 1865

Up 8 A.M. Weather fine. Salt Lake City in all its glory of Mud Slop, equaling Chicago in its earliest days. Sidewalks here are but another name for mud puddles of various degrees of advancement, some merely destroying all vestage of polish from "Cuffy's goods," others coating boots and Pants and coat. The latter is in a spotted degree, gradually deepning as it descends. The cloud foggs are very fine. Rising between the city and the mountains they cover the center of the Mountains from view leaving the Peaks & base in view. The effect is as of Peaks of all shapes & sizes, having a foundation in clouds. The air is very clear and the view looking towards the valley of the Jordan is very beautifull.

FEBRUARY 5, 1865

Attended the services held today for the third time in the hall occupied by the young men's association over Daft's store[15] and gratuitously tendered by them for the purpose. Religious services under the management of Rev. Mr. [McLeod] of the congregational order,[16] the movement having for its object the establishment of an orthodox church in this city, is worthy of record, the place of meeting being a hall in which Dances are carried on each saturday night. Situated about opposite to my stand in the Billiard Saloon it is a low long whitewashed room with some dozzen American flags arranged as curtains and ornaments. The pulpit is a platform having a body composed of a frame upon which another large flag is stretched. At two o'clock today I was privileged to assist in organizing a Sunday School. About thirty children and about a dozen young men and four teachers were present. Attended Mormon church 17th ward evening. Rough house. Rougher people.

FEBRUARY 6, 1865

Took first lesson in drawing today. Mr. Ottinger the teacher charges $15 for 20 lessons.

FEBRUARY 7, 1865

Completed first sketch today. Teacher pronounced it very good.

FEBRUARY 12, 1865

Up at 8 o'clock. Attended church in Daft's hall 11 till 12

[15] Alexander Daft had a sizable general store that regularly advertised in the *Deseret News*.

[16] Regarding Protestants in Utah at this time see Daniel S. Tuttle, *Reminiscences of a Missionary Bishop* (New York, 1906), 101–17. This minister was Rev. Norman McLeod, a Congregationalist and the main non-Mormon Protestant preacher in Utah before 1866.

A.M. Sunday school 2 P.M. Good bible class. Almost determined to close business on Sundays. 8 P.M. finds me writing these lines. Very homesick last night. Attended theatre. Ticket, $1.35. Play was "The Fool's Revenge." Mrs. Clawson, Brigham's daughter, was the Queen Page. Poor house. In wrong seat and was ejected. Found the change to my own seat the worse. Very fine day. Marched down to the end of Market Street.

FEBRUARY 19, 1865

Up at 9 A.M. Kept my resolution to close Sundays. Stayed closed all day. Snow storm all night and all day today. Only ventured out for the purpose of attending bible class. Found the door of the Hall closed. No meeting on account of the storm. Spent the day in reading "Frank Farlegh" by Smedley and "Lewis Arundell" by the same author. Both works of very superior merits.[17]

FEBRUARY 20, 1865

Up at 7½ o'clock. Business very fair. Profits $6.00 over expenses. Clipped the following from a San Francisco paper.

> A company has been formed in Pennsylvania with a million dollars capital to make sugar and syrup from corn under Professor Goeseling's patent, the Professor selling out his claim for six hundred thousand dollars. It is said that experiments have already succeeded in the production of three and a half gallons of syrup from a bushel of corn.

In 1863 I met this Professor in Buffalo, N. Y. and made a verbal agreement that for and in consideration of my advancing $100 to enable him to get his patent, and my advancing funds to build works, I should possess one half interest in all profits accruing from his discovery. No written agreement was made and the Pro-

---

17 Francis E. Smedley's *Frank Farlegh, or Scenes from the Life of a Private Pupil* (London, 1850) and his *Lewis Arundel, or the Railroad Life* (London, 1852) were then popular among boys in England and the United States.

fessor, from some cause unknown, saw fit to withdraw though if so minded I could easily have bound him. And so by ill luck I just missed $300,000.

FEBRUARY 21, 1865

News that Charleston surrendered arrived by telegraph. Procession of sleighs with flags. Brass band, speeches and good sleighing. Secessionists down at the mouth. Sold $150 worth of old coppers, 1000 in number, and completed the breaking up of my collection. Felt somewhat serious when thinking how many pleasant hours I had spent in collecting and studying them. Well, everything must come to an end, even cabinets of old coppers. Business tolerable.

FEBRUARY 26, 1865

Johnny Van Ness returned. Has been on a tour as one of the "Utah Minstrells" through the settlements south of here. He reports very cold weather. People mostly Jahoo's (a term here given to anyone decidedly on the "Know no manners order") and very good success, bringing back about $70.00. Attended theatre Saturday. Poor play. Mr. Martin's little girls in same seat with Johnny & I. Very pretty and I made much friends with one, Nellie, and received a kiss as proof that she liked me. Shop closed. Attended 13th Ward meeting at night. Mr. ———— spoke after the prayer. Remarks were accompanied by reading of a verse from the Book of Mormon and consisted mostly of separated assertions that he was going to occupy a high place in heaven in the manner of the Pharisee. He thanked God etc. Bishop Woolley followed.[18] Remarked that it was late and he had some business to attend to after church and he had concluded not to have choir sing. According to orders the Visiting committee had called at different houses in the Ward.[19] Some

[18] Bishop L. D. Woolley was regarded as the Gentiles' favorite churchman in Salt Lake City. Many non-Mormons attended his ward meeting. He went out of his way to accommodate them and did not take his religion too seriously. Thomas Stenhouse, *The Rocky Mountain Saints* (Salt Lake City, 1904), 701, 705.

[19] The visiting committee were ward teachers who were expected to visit

had insulted them. The Bishop wanted it distinctly understood that whoever insulted them insulted him and he would not fellowship them and would use his influence to prevent the church from fellowshipping them. In one or two houses there were girls courting Gentiles. When the committee called they would run away. [He said] I would not tell you all I know because you would not believe it. He wanted to take a vote that if Mr. ———— did not make his submission within one week to the authority of the church that he be expelled. All those in favor were asked to hold up their right hand. This carried.

FEBRUARY 28, 1865

Hired a room of Mr. ———— in the thirteenth ward in the house next to the assembly rooms at $30 per month. Purchased a bed, tables, chairs, dishes, curtains, wood, etc. and worked hard all day getting them to my room.

MARCH 1, 1865

Up at 8½ o'clock. Slept for first time in my new room last night. Johnny cooked and the coffee was decidedly tasteless. Griddle cakes he compounded were a veritable man trap, closing both the mouth and the digestive organs but withal they were of good size from "top to bottom." The eggs were my effort and being almost impossible to fry into anything *but* eggs they were pronounced edible by John & myself, satisfying hunger mostly by looking at the victuals. I tended trade untill relieved by Davis. Could not get my boots on in consequence of wetting them "through and through." Piled our wood in the room mostly under the bed. Spent the evening reading "The Prairie Flower" by Aimard after completing which and voting Aimard a bore, I retired.[20]

---

each family in the ward once per month. They held prayer, followed by instruction of spiritual and temporal character.

[20] Gustave Aimard, *The Prairie Flower: A Tale of the Indian Border* (London, 18—).

MARCH 2, 1865

Spent the larger part of the day fixing curtains to our windows. Finished fixing room and pronounced it all O.K.

MARCH 3, 1865

Up at 9¼ o'clock. Breakfasted on Beefsteak, fried eggs, fried potatoes and coffee. Very good. Discharged Davis and made the following "arrangements" for the government which will show my present mode of living.

1. Johnny & Davis at 8 A.M.
2. I wash and go to the stand.
3. Johnny cooks breakfast, eats & comes to stand
4. I go to breakfast, eat, and practice drawing untill 2 o'clock when I take a lesson.
5. Three o'clock I or John cook dinner which occupies 3 hours. The last one eating cleans dishes. One remains at the stand and the other at the room during the evening—Sundays excepted.

MARCH 4, 1865

President's Inauguration. Up at 8 o'clock. Opened stand & concluded to keep it open all day but changed my mind and closed about 10 o'clock. Grand celebration. About 300 infantry, 75 cavalry, and 6 field pieces from Camp Douglass. The provost guard consisting of one company, 1300 of Brigham's infantry,[21] 200 cavalry, various civic societies, mayor, staff officers, Genl. Conner & civilians in sleighs formed a procession accompanied by two Brass bands. A speaker's stand was erected in front of the Market house and the exercises were as follows: Prayer by the Congregationalist Minister. Speech by chief justice of the territory & Capt. Hooper.[22] The exercises went off well and in good

---

[21] This was the territorial militia, sometimes called the "Nauvoo Legion."

[22] William H. Hooper was the territorial delegate to Congress. He was a river-boat captain on the Mississippi River before coming to Utah, hence the title.

order. The most notable feature of the day was Brigham's troops. A more uncouth, undisciplined, and ragged set of men one could hardly imagine. They carried every variety of weapon known to civilized nations from a flint-lock single hand shot gun to the Enfield rifles bought at Camp Floyd.[23] The horses resembled the guns, the cavalry arms resembled the horses, and the men matched the kit to perfection. It is a matter of general [interest] that a people so well known to be hostile to the government and favourably inclined toward the South should turn out with so much display to celebrate the inauguration of Lincoln. It is supposed that some secret motive impelled them as their guns were said to be loaded. Having spent very heavily, $7.00 today, opened stand in the evening.

MARCH 5, 1865

Up 9 o'clock. Attended Sunday School and was "seized" & compelled to teach a class of youngsters. Attended church in the evening, inducing John to accompany me to the Hall.

MARCH 7, 1865

Quite a snow storm. Walking horrible to say the least.

MARCH 9, 1865

Took sick during the night. Could not go up street in the morning. Sick headache, fever, cold, and sore eye. Staid in my room all day. Feeling very miserable. Weather fine.

MARCH 10, 1865

Felt somewhat better this morning. Slept some during the night. Went up street and opened up shop. Staid around untill 3 o'clock when, feeling quite sick, I returned to our room. Slept

23 This is a rare description of the controversial territorial militia. In 1858–61 several thousand federal troops had been stationed at Camp Floyd, forty miles southwest of Salt Lake City, during the occupation of Utah. When the troops left for the East, the Mormons purchased an estimated $1,000,000 worth of government supplies for $40,000, among which may have been the rifles mentioned.

a little & got better. Ate a piece of toast & an egg, all I have eaten in 60 hours. Weather very fine. Walking horrible.

MARCH 25, 1865

Heavy fall of snow last night. Cold, windy, blustering day, snow falling all forenoon. Wind busy piling it in drifts. No sun, very unpleasant. Clear at 10 o'clock, snow melting rain at 5 P.M. Snow at 6 P.M. About eight inches of snow fell during the night. Johnny attended theatre. Spent the evening in Billiard Stand reading Burton's "City of the Saints."[24] Bill Hickman, a character robber freely mentioned in the work, happened to come into the Billiard Room [and] I showed him the account about him and invited him to give me a true statement concerning the three deaths which Burton alledges that he confessed to.[25] He seemed much amused, wondered how such an account ever found its way into the book, and stated that when Johnston's army[26] were out here he had command of an independent company with the right of taking as many men as he wanted from the Mormon soldiers for any raid or scout he wished to undertake. His orders were not to kill a man unless in self defense and his duty was principally and almost entirely running off the stock belonging to the army, especially the horses. He was to annoy them [the soldiers and teamsters of the Federal Army] as much as possible with a view of making them "come to terms." He says: "Now I think as much of my life as any man and would not risk it any sooner than any man, but when I could see a chance I used to take it and they thought from that that I was a terrible

24 Richard F. Burton's *The City of the Saints* (New York, 1862) was the most famous contemporary commentary on the Mormons. Written by the translator of the *Arabian Nights Tales,* it was published internationally in many languages and editions.

25 See William A. Hickman, *Brigham's Destroying Angel* (Salt Lake City, 1872, 1904), a lurid account of Hickman's adventures as a hatchet man for Brigham Young, supposedly written by himself. Hickman was a member of the Mormon force which sought to intercept federal troops in 1857–58 during the Utah War. As noted in the introduction, Miller's is a markedly different view of Hickman than that found in other accounts.

26 Colonel Albert Sidney Johnston, of later Civil War fame, commanded the federal troops that marched into Utah Territory in 1857–58.

desperado and my name was in all the eastern papers. After a while they (the church) thought I was too fast and helped to bring on the ill-feeling between the Mormons and the government so I made up my mind I would in future go along just as usual tending to my own affairs." He also took a commission from the government to apprehend horse thieves. In 1851 he fought Indians in the Humboldt and saw in one place 16 men women and children piled together that had been massacred by the Indians. He supposed he had killed a great many Indians in one day. He had 13 fighting men under him on that trip and killed 16 Indians in one day during a fight with 60 [of them]. Did not know how many Indians he had killed but "It was as many as anyone." He also shot 5 at separate times with his own hands. His business under his commission led him of necessity into many scrapes with the thieves. He said: "They used to come down and steal horses. We would start after them and bring them and the horses back again and sometimes we would bring the horses without them." The gestures with which he accompanied the last words left no doubt as to what he had done with them.

Speaking of the Danites,[27] he said there was a body calling themselves Danites during the troubles in Missouri but there never was an association of that kind in this country. He said that his chief difficulty and the cause for all his troubles was in his sympathy with men who had got into trouble at one time. He was trying to clear a young man and in spite of all he could do they sent him to the Penitentiary. He then went to the judge of the Supreme Court to get out a writ of habeas corpus. The judge asked him why he did not release all the prisoners. Acting upon the suggestion he [Hickman] released every prisoner, instead of one, some 9 in number, "for sport." He now holds a commission from Genl. Connor for apprehending horse thieves. Bill Hickman is a thick-set man about 5 ft. 4 in. high. His face

27 The Danites were a group of independent Mormons who sought to redress grievances suffered at the hands of Missourians during the Mormon "persecutions" of the 1830's.

is very full and also very red, owing undoubtedly to the mixed cause of whiskey and exposure. Blue eyes, roman nose, dark brown hair, thick full neck. He looks like a Blackleg and at the same time has an expression of good humor upon his face. He often comes into the Billiard Rooms to drink.

APRIL 6, 1865

Snow storm during the night. Morning cold. Drizzly snow. Today first day of the convention.[28] I did not reach the Tabernacle until 10½ o'clock A.M. about half an hour late. The convention is held semi-monthly on the 6, 7, 8th of April and the 6, 7, 8th of October and consists of the assembling together of the Saints from all parts of the country as far as possible for the purpose of electing officers, missionaries, & transacting other general business pertaining to the church. At this time of year the meetings are held in the Tabernacle which is a building resembling very much an inverted scow. The following is a ground plan of the building: [reproduced opposite page 40.] Heber C. Kimball had the stand when I entered.[29] In person he is of the Abe Lincoln order, tall, gaunt & boney, his manner of speaking is a sort of vulgar talking, rambling discourse in the course of which he often starts in a sentence at a terrible yell and delivers the last three or four words in a voice so low that it is inaudible at a distance of 20 feet. He is decidedly uneducated and I presume, owing to the realization of the fact, he confines himself mostly to remarks, or rather to attacks, not particularly characterized by either moderation or decency.

Heber C. Kimball's Discourse

I am going to have a new tabernacle. When I get my new tabernacle you would not know but [what] I had a new body. We ought to be the happiest people in the

[28] The official name for this gathering, still held twice a year, is the General Conference of the Church of Jesus Christ of Latter-day Saints.

[29] Kimball was Brigham Young's First Counsellor in the powerful First Presidency of the Mormon Church.

world. We are the happiest people on the face of the earth.
The world don't love us and don't respect us. Jesus said
I call you out of the world and the world will hate and
despise you. They that are not of you are against you. We
are the most blessed people on the earth. How many times
has President Young declared when the Holy Ghost was
upon him that we are the most blessed people on the earth.
We have representatives here from almost every nation
on the face of the earth. Not much difference in our out-
looks. The trees of the forest and the leaves on the trees
look very much alike and yet no two are alike. So with
the church. Though our forms & faces may be very different, yet we all belong to the tree [of] Zion. But should
we differ not the least should I be at difficulty and variance
one with the other. I say nay (loud). Every branch should
be one. I look upon my family and children [and] if they
are like unto one it is because they do as I tell them (and
that is the only way to get the attributes of God as revealed
through Jesus). The man that takes the course to steal—
is that the attribute of our father? Stealing or lying is not
the attribute of our father. Why do you do it? Brother
Heber, Brother Brigham, when I speak these things I
don't know any better. I think of a good many things I
can not speak about. I am alive (loud). Jesus lives. My
father lives, the Holy Ghost lives, and that is the reason
I live. There is just one course for me to take. That is to
live for myself. It is for me to live alone and independent
—as if there was no other man on earth—a life of holiness.
President Young would, like me, live as holy a life as
Jesus. Daniel asked no odds of them when he opened
the[?] to pray. Not even [?] stood up for him. Here we
have a revelation (holding up the book). I am as full of
revelation as this book. What use are these books without
revelation? Joseph, I heard him say that when he gave
revelations and the people received it and understood it

like himself, that they had the spirit of revelation. Am I troubled? I am not troubled by a great many things. And a great many things I let trouble me. I yield to them. It affects me. I want to have confidence in a man. If he tells me a story and if I receive what he says and it's a cursed lie I am influenced by what he says. I go to my next neighbor and I hold him at a distance because of the spirit I received from that damned scoundrel.

I want to know if blood, war, and destruction will come upon the United States because they consented to the death of Joseph Smith. They called him a deceiver and a bastard but he did not come that way (laughter). We all come that way I suppose. Well now excuse me. I don't know of anything better for anyone than to laugh.

Everything was made desolate in the United States because they killed Joseph Smith. I have brethren who have been preaching against me for years. Why, I have not committed any crime. What does it prove? Something [is] wrong. We say we are poor, weak mortals. The more I hear of his life and intelligence the more I see I am a poor weak mortal. I am as weak as the weakest thing in the world. Consider the apples and fruit. They grow and blossom. And yet one frost sends them back to mother earth. Yokes of oxen in the desert will go and find water. The revelation which God has put in their breast tells them where to go. Look at us, poor pencilmen who keep driving each other to death for pieces of paper not worth half the fuss. I have not got language like some of us, brethern. You come here and stretch your necks for hours and [even] then don't know what I mean. It is good to laugh. Jesus taught laughter. He went and sat down with the publicans and sinners who took their hale[?] and wine and laughed among the merriest of men on the face of the earth. Brethren this is the first day of conference. When I think of paying 60¢ a yard for the poorest piece of callico which when washed twice there is nothing left of it— (Aside): Spose I talk a little about these things. Brother Brigham, would it be out of the way? Brigham: Not at all! In the days of my youth we had what was called shirting. Take the cloth we had then, it would wear out 4 yds. of what we have now. It wasent because it was not so light but it would pull up and pull up and a shirt would last a year. Women now days are smarter than they were in those days, at least they think so. I went a courting in those days. I wanted to court my wife in proper style so I bought her a dress before I married her. It took 5 yds. in those days. A man could tell what he got in those days. Now you can't tell how much is under there (motions). You know what, I feel kind of nice and child like (voice: Feel cold?) No, I feel kind of warm. Do you know where I have departed from the truth? I have a good feeling toward Latter day Saints. Don't talk to me about the Saint that don't pray. I heard President Young. I know that he is a Prophet. You throw him off. Those men that do not take a course to build up the Kingdom of God, I can say in the name of God they will go down. Now I hear things. You carry off things and you think Brother Heber does things that he don't do. We're apostles. We're called through Heaven to our calling. Brother Brigham knows how I feel about coming to the tabernacle and taking cold for 14 years. Brother Brigham, Brother Kimball, [people ask], why don't you go heal the sick? We can't do it. But we can go into our room, which is pure and not desecrated, where we can pray for them. The air is purer there than in any room except Brigham's.[30]

30 The *Deseret News* for April 12, 1865, carried this discourse in abbreviated form. Miller's version is also shortened but on the whole brutally accurate. The more vulgar remarks of Kimball's addresses were never printed in official church organs, including the *Journal of Discourses*. Miller's account is, therefore, unique in its color. Mormon sermons typically covered a wide range of subjects, both spiritual and temporal, and were delivered by officials who were also laymen. Kimball had been a New England potter who became a farmer and miller.

Rockfellow store where Miller worked, Virginia City, Montana Territory, 1865.

Miller at Virginia City, Montana Territory, 1865.

Address by *Geo. A. Smith,* Apostle[31]

It is the 35th year since the commencement of the organization of the church and we are assembled here to transact business pertaining to the building up of the temple of Zion. It is really true, as expressed by Elder Kimbal, that a good many saints, men and for aught I know, women do take measures and pursue a course directly opposite to the course marked out by the authorities of the church. Something [is] in the human mind so peculiarly organized that we can not foresee the result. We hear it said that we must lay up grain for 7 years. It has been predicted that there will be a famine of 7 years. The time has got to come when all the saints must all be rich without going to the devil in consequence. If in the acquisition of this wealth a system of lying is resorted to, the spirit of the Lord is withdrawn and he is left to worship the worldly things. When a man in business begins to sacrifice little principles, let him be alarmed. Not until we are properly christened are the riches of the earth ours. But that schooling may be long.

APRIL 15, 1865

News this morning of the assassination of President Lincoln. Such a general feeling of Horror, grief, and indignation I never before witnessed and never expect to witness again. At 10 o'clock stores closed. Billiard Saloon closed. During the day a couple of men arrested at Camp Douglass for expressing joy at Lincoln's death.

APRIL 20, 1865

Closed according to orders of President Johnson. At 12 o'clock services in the tabernacle commenced. Order of exercises as follows:

[31] Smith, one of the original Twelve Apostles of the Mormon church, was a leading colonizer in southern Utah. He became a member of the "First Presidency" when Kimball died in 1868.

Prayer	J. D. Richards (Mormon)
Address	Amasa Lyman (Do.)
Singing by choir	
Eulogy of life of Pres. Lincoln by A. McLeod (gentile)	

The address of Lyman was very good and McLeod delivered a discourse emphasizing merit. The finest I have ever heard. Everything went off orderly and agreeable. Soldiers and Mormons for once laid aside the feelings of animosity and met for a common purpose.

APRIL 23, 1865

Up at 11 o'clock. Attended bible class as usual after which Johnny Van Ness and I strolled down to Jordan Bridge. Weather delightfull. Arrived at our quarters at 8½ o'clock quite worn out. Finished "Martin Chuzzlewit" by Charles Dickens and commenced "Barnaby Rudge."

APRIL 24, 1865

Trade horribly dull. Not paying expenses.

APRIL 25, 1865

Billiard Room closes tomorrow. Having concluded to give up my stand worked during the evening with Johnny moving goods & cases from the Billiard Room to Chad & Davis. Got everything moved.

APRIL 26, 1865

Recd. a short letter from Julia today. After considerable hesitation I made up my mind to write to her. Spent the greater portion of the day in writing a letter. It growing dark I went up the street with Johnny. Meeting some young men who invited us to bathe in the Warm Sulphur spring, one of the party having provided a wagon. It was quite dark when we arrived and decidedly cool. The water was delightfull. After bathing as long as was agreeable we started home again. After narrowly escaping upsetting several times we arrived in the city about 8½ o'clock. Owing to my wetting my stockings I was unable to get my boots on and had to walk two or three long blocks in my stockings. After writing a letter untill 12 o'clock I retired.

APRIL 30, 1865

Johnny and I attended theatre last night. Play was Macbeth by William Shakespeare and he was truly "murdered." It was decidedly void of merit. John & I in the course of a disputation, becoming excited, got into high words & abuse this morning. I was still wroth and would listen to no advances which Johnny made. Spent the afternoon in scrubbing pots, kettles, etc., preparatory to vacating my room. Johnny brought his horse to the house, strapped his blankets, frying pan, etc., to the saddle, & started for Virginia City, Montana. When first starting his horse threw him off some ten or fifteen feet. A second attempt was more successful for I saw no more of him after a cold shake of the hand. I have determined to give my opinion of Johnny. His bad qualities are chiefly an almost total want of delicacy or consideration for another's peculiar feelings and a terrible large development of selfishness. His morality is of a very inferior quality and only the question of expediency would prevent him, were the opportunity offered, from doing a great many things both unlawful & wrong. His good qualities are a love of home and relatives, a tolerable strong resolution, some energy, an affectionate temperament, a small quantity of pride. As a man I do not like him. He being quick and impulsive, and I also, we were constantly agreeing to disagree.

MAY 1, 1865

Commenced boarding at City Hotel after batching for two months. My conclusion in regard to batching is that it "don't pay." Board at City Hotel is $13 per week, including bed. Spent most of the day in dragging a handcart through the city with Bed, bedding, dishes, furniture etc. from our room. House [is] kept by James Miller who is a nephew of Cornelius Miller of Amsterdam, N. Y. Had a dance in the evening, music by one of the boarders fiddling. Was highly entertained but did not participate in the dancing. Mr. Miller's two daughters and two strange girls carried on that branch of the biz [business].

MAY 6, 1865

Mr. Waggerman and myself started to ascend mountain. Reached the summit after 3½ hours through sage brush and mosquitoes. At the summit a party of school children from the 14th Ward had planted a flag. The view of the valley was grand but was much impeded by swarms of mosquitoes. Built a fire of sagebrush and lay down in the smoke quite comfortable. After remaining at the summit a while we started down the mountain at the same time that the picnic party started out from the foot of it. They looked very pretty. There were in all about 85, mostly small boys and old girls. They carried appropriate flags & banners. Found a water canteen going up. Attached it to the flag staff. On our way down we visited the Cave seen from the city and found the larger part to consist of a mouth. The Indians often lived in it for days. Visited the sulpher springs but did not bathe.

MAY 7, 1865

A lady, one of Mr. Miller's daughters, soliciting the company of two other gentlemen and myself for a promenade, we complied and walked through some of the principal streets of the city. Our party were continually dogged by about a dozzen of the self-constituted men who have been following every person found in the streets lately with a lady. I determined to show them up in the Vedette.[32]

MAY 8, 1865

Finished my "article" today. A doctor from San Francisco who is stopping at the City Hotel and myself rode horseback to

[32] The *Daily Union Vedette* was begun by General Patrick E. Connor at Camp Douglas. See J. Cecil Alter, *Early Utah Journalism* (Salt Lake City, 1938), 55, 67, 333, 340, 342–43, 361–75. A copy is reproduced on page 67 of the work.

Camp Douglas. Called at the Vedette office. After a short conversation with Mr. Livingston we left the article. Rode to the cemetery after which we rode to the Hot Springs situated about four miles from town. Returned to the city at 3 P.M. Several policemen had called for me during my absence. Met them in the street afterwards. They pronounced the actions of the young men as unauthorized and wished for information that would lead to their conviction.

MAY 9, 1865

My article appeared in the Vedette today as follows:[33]

MAY 18, 1865

After waiting for Lieut. Miller to pay me a balance of $169 due me for two weeks, I this day contracted 2500 lbs. to be taken to Virginia City at $10 in gold. Without the sum due from Lieut. Miller I could not make out the amount. After waiting untill 5 o'clock I started for Camp Douglas. Walked there in 60 minutes. Found the Lieut., collected the money, and started for town, reaching there in 35 minutes, a distance of 3½ miles. Made an arrangement with a young fellow (Camel) to walk to Virginia City, 450 miles. He today backed out, I wishing to go & he not. Supper of bread & milk.[34]

MAY 19, 1865

Up at 7. Spent the forenoon in getting 300 doz. eggs packed, carrying boxes, eggs, etc., Tom Waggoman very kindly assisting me, got ready 660 doz. and shipped them.

[33] Miller attached to his diary a clipping dated May 8, 1865, signed "A Gentleman," which protested the treatment of Gentiles by "fanatical" Mormons on the streets of Salt Lake City: "How long shall it be said that the nation, so long recognized as the protector of freedom, allows its citizens to be so grossly insulted by a body of fanatics?" his remarks read.

[34] Miller's departure from Salt Lake City, and that of several acquaintances, was connected with the boycott against non-Mormon merchants which began late in 1865. He was steadily losing money before his departure from Salt Lake City and the Mormons were becoming increasingly hostile to Gentile merchants like himself.

MAY 21, 1865

Took my traps to Mr. Waggoman's house as my week's board expired last evening & I start for Virginia City tomorrow & do not care to commence another week. Shipped 660 doz. eggs yesterday to Johnny at Virginia City. All the Mormon police are decidedly down on me since my article in the Vedette. I am decidedly tiard of Salt Lake City and the Mormons and long to leave them.

MAY 22, 1865

Finished purchasing my outfit with which I intend to *walk* to Virginia City, a distance of over 400 miles. It consists of: 14 lbs. Bacon, 3 lbs. Coffee, 4 lbs. Sugar, one $25 paper [?] of pepper, $10 worth of salt (1 lb.), 18 lbs. flour, a horse, cost $90, Saddle, one pr. California blankets, an overcoat & suit of clothes I have on (consisting of pants and vest foxed & linen coat, shirt, 4 pr. linen stockings), towel & a pillow which I happened to have, a pint tin cup, tin plate, knife, fork, and spoon. Our party consists of four persons besides myself. Two young men, about 25. Gus ———— from Missouri, ———— from Iowa, Mr. Grey from near Buffalo, N. Y., & Mr. Crane from St. Lawrence Co., the two last aged respectively 40 and 50 years. They are complete strangers to me and I have concluded to go with them for the very reason that they have "Nary [a] Red [cent]" and will be sure to walk it. Find it difficult to get company. Started about 3 o'clock. Walked about 10 miles and camped about a mile east or south of Sessions.[35] Fine weather. Eggs, bacon, bread, and coffee for supper.

MAY 23, 1865

Horses lost last night in the mountains. Up at daybreak and with Gus went to look for them. Tracked them three miles, lost track and I found them about a mile further on. Arrived at camp about 8 o'clock. Ate breakfast, packed horses, and started.

[35] Sessions Settlement was the pioneer name for the present-day suburb of Salt Lake City, Bountiful.

Reached Farmington, a town of 500 inhabitants, a distance of 10 miles, about noon. Camped, cooked bacon, potatoes, coffee, and bread. Found that the bridge over the Weber River, by usual route of travel, is so surrounded by water that it is impassable. After traveling 20 miles we are camped 5 miles from Ogden. I am writing this in camp by campfire. It rained two or three times today while we were on the march, hardly enough to wet us. Last 10 miles of our walk today was through heavy sand. Reaching the Weber river found it was so high that the river had broken out in a new channel over which a bridge has been erected about twelve feet long where the modest charge of 50¢ for man and horse and $2.00 for wagon was preferred. Country fine farming land, mostly cultivated. Crossed a great many streams of clear sparkling water, very refreshing. Passed a number of Mormon villages. At the lowest calculation I have walked 38 miles today.

MAY 24, 1865

Made up my bed under some oak bushes but I got the idea of snakes into my head and that, with the aching of my bones throughout my body, prevented my sleeping any. Up about an hour after daylight. My horse strayed into the mountains. Walked two miles among the hills but could not find him. Came across a great many beautifull flowers, some of them very fragrant— especially a white lilly.[36] Land very much cut up with hills and gullies. Returning to camp found that one of the boys had caught my horse and was busy packing horses. Reached Ogden, a place of about 1500 inhabitants, about 11 o'clock. Blacksmith asked $8 to shoe my horse. As I had not that much money I could not have him shod. Got my boots mended. Walked about three miles from Ogden & camped. Dined on bread & coffee. Water poor and warm. Walked to Willow Creek.[37] I was about a quarter of a mile ahead of the rest & stopping at the mail station [when]

[36] Probably the Sego lily, Utah's state flower. Early pioneers ate the bulbs of this flower during periods of famine.
[37] A small settlement fourteen miles north of Ogden now called Willard.

the stage drove up. Mr. Halsey,[38] Mr. Thomas, and two other acquaintances were in the stage bound for Virginia City. Mr. Halsey gave me an introduction to a gentleman who he said would give me some employment on my reaching "the City," in consequence of which I am in very good spirits tonight. Camp in centre of the town. I am to sleep with the goods and the rest of the boys sleep with the horses, which are picketed in a field about 1/2 mile from where we camp. Made 22 miles today.

MAY 25, 1865

Slept very little, dogs prowling around. Country around here very good. Willow Creek contains about 300 inhabitants, quite hard. Last night got a job for one of the men cooking for a train of 6 wagons. Wages $20.00 for trip. This leaves four of us. Passed the Point of Rocks yesterday where at the foot of a mountain there are 12 to 15 hot springs very strongly impregnated with what one of the boys called "copper as water," so hot that I could not hold my finger in them 10 seconds. The soil covered in some places with salt. Up about daybreak, built a fire. A short time afterwards the boys came up from the meadow. After breakfasting we walked to Brigham City where there are perhaps a 1000 people and some very comfortable houses. A large commodious building standing by the roadside in an open square is used for courthouse, church school and theatre. Bought about 1/2 a bushel of potatoes at $2.25 pr. Bush. Leaving Brigham City we tramped 10 miles when we came to a large body of water, a Pond supplied by some invisible springs with very good water. Dined on bread and water as there is no wood. The last of the 17 mile walk before dinner was a heaping measure for me. Started at about 3 o'clock. Came to a small hollow at which, situated a few feet apart, were four springs, one very hot salt water, one cold salt water, one cold sweet water (soft) and one cold hot water—all running into one channell. Shortly after I killed two rattlesnakes. Great many crickets in the road, some

38 W. L. Halsey was an agent for Ben Holladay's Overland Mail and Express Company and operated a station near present-day Collinston, Utah.

an inch and a half long. Arrived within two miles of Bear River. Washed a pair of stockings. Mosquitoes very thick and ferocious. Supper of boiled potatoes, bacon, bread and "Nevada Tea." Great numbers of snakes in this country. Grass magnificent. Cooked with sagebrush. Made 25 miles today.

MAY 26, 1865

Could not sleep during the night. Was cold. Up at daybreak and built a fire to warm myself. Started at about 6 o'clock. Crossed Overland Stage's Ferry, or "Upper Ferry"[39] [which] charges $1 for man and horse. Roads good. Camped at station 12 miles from Bear River, making a walk of 17 miles before dinner. Was very tiard before we reached water. My feet in poor condition, between blood blisters and rubbing. Bear River is 85 miles from Salt Lake City. At Bear River we first entered Malade Valley.[40] Very hot day. Walked about 5 miles from the station and camped on a hillside looking down on the Malade. Very pleasant spot. Bear River Mountains on both sides of us. As I write this the mosquitoes are so thick and troublesome that I can hardly write a line. We are now 102 miles from Gt. Salt Lake City. The sun is set and with that exception all nature seems to be resting after a weary day's work. I write this lying on my bed, which is simply my overcoat thrown on the ground. The voices of Gray, Crane, Gus, and another party of four men who have a team and wagon, come to my ear and just now from Gus comes the inquiry, "Do the mosquitoes trouble you?" Wood about a mile from camp. Grass fine. Made 22 miles today.

MAY 27, 1865

Started at 7½ o'clock. Slept better last night. Took my pil-

39 Near Honeyville, Utah.

40 The "shortest river in the world," possibly only three or four miles in length, and spelled Malad today, this stream was named by French-Canadian trappers who were possibly made ill by drinking its water too rapidly. Works Progress Administration, *Idaho: A Guide in Word and Pictures* (Caldwell, Idaho, 1937), 213, 246.

low, which is stuffed with wool, cut it in two parts, put my feet into them, fastened them with cords to my legs, and started walking. Made 12 miles and camped at an Overland Station. Dinner coffee, sorghum, & bread. Reached a new settlement just preparing to cultivate their land. Camped among the Bluffs after leaving Malade Valley. Very windy. Ate about as much dust as victuals. Baked my first loaf of bread, very good. One part of my pillow gave out and I had to walk a mile in my stockings. Terribly tiard when I reached camp. Supper bread, coffee, & boiled potatoes. We are now 128 miles from Salt Lake City. Fine country. Large droves of cattle & horses. Gus killed 3 rattlesnakes in the road where we made our beds. Passed a curious formation this afternoon. About 50 yds. from the road a circular mass of Deposit of lime much resembling petrified moss is formed into a ridge like the side of a fountain, enclosing a boggy piece of grass & water.[41] Made 26 miles today.

MAY 28, 1865

Up at daybreak. Cut my boots and walked in them about 15 miles & camped. Passed a herding ranch. Followed Marsh river and entered Marsh valley. Camped on Marsh creek, left it and walked 5 miles through the bluffs. Snow-capped mountains on all sides. Reached Marsh creek again. Had to roll up our pants and wade across. Followed a beautifull valley in the centre of which runs the Marsh creek, for three miles, and then struck across the hills again. About half hour before sun down reached the Port Neugh [Neuf] which is usually fordable. But, as the water is very high, a man and woman have squatted here & erected the customary bridge of timber covered with willow sticks and charged $4 for passage of myself and horse. I gave out about half a mile from the Bridge and had to rest a few moments before I could proceed. We walked today 30 miles. Party of Indians camped near the Bridge—two families.

41 The Malad River is fed largely by such subterranean springs which dot central Idaho. WPA, *Idaho Guide*, 247.

MAY 29, 1865

Talked about an hour last evening seated around the camp fire. Two Indians in the party, each with a squaw. They had been together about a month. One Bannock and the rest Snake Indians. They had stolen the squaws, very pretty little bodies being about as large as a 14 year old child. Had beautifull eyes & hair of "jetty Black" and were very quiet, saying nothing whatever—not even smiling until I held a looking glass before one of them. A smile repaid my efforts. Gave one of them a cup of sugar, half a pint for a pair of moccasins & a piece of Bread for showing me how to tie them. Saw sand hill cranes, wild geese, ducks, & plover. Caught 2 trout yesterday. Slept cold as usual, having nothing under me & only one blanket over me. Was first up, built fire, put potatoes on & cut Ham. Made discovery that skin peeling off my nose, effects of sun. Concluded to walk in my moccasins. Started at 5 o'clock and walked untill 12 o'clock. Camped on a creek. Very dusty victuals. Made 20 miles, the longest walk made yet at one time. I gave out about a mile from camp. Had to sit down & rest. After resting walked into camp where I arrived with feet blistered and swollen, not able to stand. With my resolution to walk all the way to Virginia City considerably shaken inasmuch as someone rides one of the horses all the while & the boys press me to ride very often. After washing my feet in the stream awhile I reformed my resolutions though it is *terrible tough*. A party of ox-teamsters are camped a few hundred yards from us & a fiddle is busily "discoursing sweet music." Sun terrible hot. A slight wind keeps us from danger of sunstroke. No more settlements or ranches. Crossed a great number of streams caused by melting of snow. Over one of them a party of Indians had felled a tree and demanded toll. I gave them an old pocket match box. Gus filled it with matches and our toll was paid. After resting about an hour we started again. About a mile from camp I met Mr. Miner of the firm of Hadley & Miner[42] of Salt Lake. They owe me $180, which is probably as near as they will ever get to paying it to me. He rode

[42] Aurelius Miner was a prominent Mormon merchant and freighter.

an Indian Poney and stated that Pocatello's squaw had stolen two Indian Ponies from him & he had been following them for two weeks unsuccessfully however. Followed the Port Neuf for a mile & left it. Passed a spring of fine water on the right of the road about four miles from the river. Walked to Dry Creek 7 miles from the River where the boys had already camped. Was decidedly used up. Washed feet and stockings. Ate supper, rolled my blankets around me, & slept. Walked 27 miles today.

MAY 30, 1865

Up about daybreak. Slept well for the first time since leaving the city. Gus took the shoes off my horse. He was very factious and came very near striking me with his hoofs several times. Walked to Ross Fork, 14 miles & across the sand plain to Blackfoot Ferry 13 miles, walking 27 miles without stopping, the longest single walk we have yet made. The only drink we had was at Ross's Fork. Camped in a fine place on Blackfoot River & dined. It is said that on this river the Mormons first settled and were driven off by the Indians.[43] My feet are getting slightly better. Very hot today. Saw Humboldt desert in the distance. The boys are fishing and I am going to have a nap by the side of the stream in the shadow of the willows. Started at 5 o'clock & walked to Middle Ferry on Snake river 5 miles, which makes 32 miles walked today. Camped across the river. Charge for ferry 50¢ man & horse. We meet Snake & Bannack Indians every hour. As I write there are about 15 around me, among them "Bannock Jim."[44]

MAY 31, 1865

Sleeping very cold, I arose before day light to build a fire to warm myself. Got breakfast and started up the road along [the] Snake River. Walked untill 11 o'clock through rolling,

43 Miller mistakes this area for the Salmon River Mission begun by Mormons at Fort Lemhi in 1855 in the upper valley of the Salmon River Basin.

44 In January, 1863, some three hundred Bannack Indians were killed at the Battle of Bear River by Colonel Patrick E. Connor's troops from Camp Douglas, Utah, in a foray which put an end to severe Indian troubles in southeastern Idaho.

sandy country covered with sage brushes. Walked about 20 miles and camped on hillside by slough. Started at 5½ A.M. Staid untill one o'clock, then started and travelled 17 miles; reached the Snake River at about 7 A.M. I was about used up. In all we have made today 37 miles, the "Tallest" day yet excepting one. We are now getting into the sage brush country. The Snake River is very high, having risen so as to cover the road in many places. Passed a point where the bank by the riverside was being gradually washed away.

JUNE 1st, 1865

We were treated to some very fine muddy water last evening, owing to the flood. Were also treated, after we had supped, to some very tolerable music. A party of minstrels, among them Billy Sheppard & several other acquaintances that I had formed through the medium of John Van Ness at Salt Lake City, were some Californians bringing 150 head of horses from Los Angeles, S. C. Building a rousing fire of sage brush & with a convenient pile nearby, from which to replenish, we gathered around the fire, each choosing his *peculiar* position. I, laying at full length, watched the "Mid Night Queen" and her "Starry Train" though with feelings of sadness and heartache of my former lost home and kindred. The music was not particularly select or calculated to suit a taste in the least degree fastidious. But, combined with the circumstances in which we were placed, alone with nature and nothing human save ourselves in the wilderness. . . . After listening from 8 to 11 o'clock the evening's entertainment wound up with "The Lilly of the West" and we retired to our "positions for the night." Slept very cold, or rather did not sleep at all on a/c of the cold and insufficient covering. Started about an hour after sunrise. Found myself feeling unwell and after marching about 20 miles I gave out. As the rest wanted to go on, I took what provisions I needed for 5 days. Gus, Mr. Crane, & Mr. Grey went on. As is almost invariably [the case] in "Splits" on the Plains, considerable bad feeling was shown. I am now camped alone and intend to remain alone here untill tomorrow morning.

Had to travel 10 miles today, in addition to the usual distance, the road being inundated owing to the rise in "the Snake." *Later* —changed my mind and traveled 6 miles further when, coming to the camp of the Minstrell Boys, I rested for the night. Camped on bottom, part of which is overflowed, and the rest, including the spot on which we are encamped, only a few inches above the watermark. The water, rising rapidly, we expect to find ourselves under water before morning. Had to wade through mud knee deep to get water for supper but I did sleep, which is somewhat unusual of late.

JUNE 2, 1865

Was up before daybreak, made coffee, fried ham, and with old dried bread made out a breakfast after which I packed the horse & started. Made 23 miles, mostly through a heavy, sandy country. Camped on Chamois Creek.[45] Once during the morning's walk I dropped by the roadside entirely fagged out with fatigue & thirst. My horse, poor beast, standing perfectly still almost over me, kept the sun from me. A few moments rest sufficed to enable me to proceed. Reaching Chamois Creek I managed by considerable perseverence & effort to wash my feet & cook Dinner. On examination I found my left ankle so much swollen and inflamed that I dare not continue my trip on foot. After I had been in camp several hours, Billy Sheppard's wagon comming up, I made arrangements to ride the balance of the way. Followed Chamois Creek four miles and camped near the Station. Grass poor. Slept in wagon. Billy & Jones entertained a crowd in the Station house with divers pieces on guitar & Banjo. "A drink all around" followed after which I retired to the wagon. Bought 20¢ worth of milk today from a train [?] woman. It was delicious. Feed scarce. Wood scarcer. Made 28 miles today.

JUNE 3, 1865

Was first one up. Collected some brush & chips. Got quite an early start. Had to go about 3 miles through heavy sand. My

45 Today's Camas Creek.

nose, cheeks, and chin are blistered beautifully owing to the alkali which is one of the ingredients of the soil. It strongly affects the water. Camped on Dry Creek, which is very picturesque here. The stream, which is about 20 feet high and 2 feet deep being enclosed with 2 sides of perpendicular rock from 10 to 30 feet high. It is not a permanent stream and owes its existence to melting snow on the mountain sides. Made 25 miles & camped in a Kanyon on Dry Creek. Supper bread & coffee. Wood plenty & feed good. I traded some bread for dried venison with an Indian. The Bokaria [?] horsemen, with the 150 head of horses we passed & stopped to see them throw the Lassoo & ride the wild horses. Country uneven & very hilly. Slightly homesick, an affliction by the way which I am not much troubled with *on the Plains* as there is too much work to be done and too little time to do it in. There are a number of Beaver Dams near our camp. My foot is improving rapidly.

JUNE 4, 1865

Horribly cold last night. Did not sleep an hour soundly. Everybody up early to build a fire and get warmed up. Horses gone. Cold wind today. Spent about 6 hours in hunting horses. As we were about to conclude that they were stolen, George found them about 4 miles from camp & brought them in. Finally got started & made good time. Country getting hillier. Very romantic scenery and a very splendid road. Passed the divide & made Pleasant Valley. Reached a creek & camped. I and Gofer carried some sagebrush about a mile to camp. Our grub now reduced to bread and coffee. Country very romantically laid out but filled in with poor alkali soil.

JUNE 5, 1865

Owing to my former sufferings I concluded to dispense with my exclusive notions as to sleeping alone & slept with three others on the ground. Was very uncomfortable squeezed. Very cold last night. Froze ice in the coffee pot over an inch thick and almost froze us. Slept tolerable. Crawled out about sunrise, drove up the horses that had strayed off about a half mile, ate my bread and coffee and started the wagon. Drove about 2 miles beyond Sagebrush Toll Gate. Made dinner of a cup of coffee and a small piece of bread about half enough to satisfy my hunger. Made about 40 miles. Came to a deserted log cabin with good fireplace in it which we have taken possession of and are congratulating ourselves on our extreme good fortune and on the prospect of a *night's sleep*. We are cooking the last of our bread and tomorrow's breakfast and dinner will probably be minus [it]. Passed a great many snow drifts, some only a few feet from the road, the wind blowing over which makes it sometimes very cool driving.

Miller (left) and unidentified friend, Virginia City, Montana Territory, *c.* 1865. From a tintype.

Miller (right) and friend, Bannack, Montana Territory, *c.* 1866.

III

MONTANA TERRITORY

JUNE 6, 1865

Up at sunrise & started for "the City." Made about 22 miles
& camped. Breakfasted on corned beef which one of our party got
from the horsemen. A small piece left for dinner. Arrived in
"the City" at about 5 o'clock, having had some difficulty in getting through the Toll Gate, as the toll was $10 and we had "nary
a red [cent]." Very faint, weak, weary, and homesick. Had only
$2 in my pocket. Reached the top of the divide and instead of
seeing a city I saw nothing but a collection of log cabins consti-
tuting the city of Nevada.[1] Descending the hill with our horses
on the run we crossed the gulch and entered Nevada, driving

1 Nevada City was part of Virginia City in the first years of the Alder Gulch
Rush. It was here that George Ives, among the first of the Plummer gang to meet
punishment, was hanged. The gulch between Nevada and Virginia "cities" in the
1860's was a continuous thoroughfare of claims, miners' cabins, and tents, sometimes referred to as "Lower Town."

through the only business street the place affords. Our spirits were not improved by noticing that almost every other store we passed was "To Rent." After driving about 2 miles along the gulch we suddenly came upon Virginia City situated on both sides of the gulch.[2] The stores are of a much superior order to those in Nevada City and half a doz. of them are very fine looking buildings. "Everybody and his cousin" here seems to live in a log cabin and mud roof. Our boys are all broke and I, having only $2 to stand me a month, we were a hungry looking set. One of them borrowed some money from a friend, however, and we went to an eating saloon and filled ourselves, a process of half to three quarters of an hour duration. I felt decidedly famished, not having had a square meal in four days. Sent my horse out to a ranch owned by Cook & Co. at a cost of $3.00 a month. Slept in the dirt in the Saddle & Harness room of Cook's & Co.'s Stable. Went to bed early as I felt sick. This is a very dull, desolate looking place. Did not find Johnny Van Ness here as I expected, which added considerable color to the Blues which I had.

JUNE 7, 1865

Up about sunrise according to my custom since leaving S. L. City. Walked to Nevada City to try to discover the whereabouts of Johnny Van Ness. Could not find him however. Made an arrangement by which I pledge my saddle blankets, overcoat, and horse as security untill the eggs I shipped from S. L. City[3] arrive

2 In May, 1863, one of the greatest gold discoveries in history was made at Virginia City, which, along with adjoining communities, became a town of 10,000 inhabitants within two years. The first year's yield from Alder Gulch, along which the town was located, amounted to $10,000,000 or more. Virginia City, the first incorporated town in Montana, became its second capital from 1865–76. Ultimately $120,000,000 in gold is estimated to have been taken out of Alder Gulch. When Miller arrived, Virginia City possessed a number of log cabins, a half-dozen frame houses, a few stone stores, some brush wikiups, and the Planter's House, largest of several hotels. Early firsthand accounts of Virginia City include: Arthur Jerome Dickson (ed.), *Covered Wagon Days: A Journey across the Plains in the Sixties . . . the Private Journals of Arthur Jerome Dickson* (Cleveland, 1929), 167–85; Clyde McLemore, (ed.), "Virginia City in 1864," *Frontier and Midland*, Vol. XIX (1938–39), 129–33.

3 It will be recalled that Miller had shipped 660 dozen eggs to Virginia City from Salt Lake City. Much of southern Montana's food supply came via this

and are sold, which makes it a sure thing that I will not starve, the idea of which troubled me somewhat yesterday. Paid out my last $2.00 for breakfast and dinner at the Mountain House, kept by a gentleman formerly resident of La Porte, Indiana. From him I learn that Ed Dale's brother has a claim in the gulch which he is working. Concluded that I would not hunt him up however. From Nevada's west end to the east end of Virginia City it is about 3 miles. The houses and stores are mostly on one street & are built of loggs, mud, & stones with dirt roofs. The street runs along "Virginia Gulch" where, for a width of 500 to 1000 feet, shovelled, uplifted, & piled, it looks as if an enormous Hog had been uprooting the soil. My board and lodging at the Missouri House[4] are to cost me $14 pr. week. Mr. Ray is proprietor of the establishment. "Puss" Ray, a very friendly girl, is one of the *attractions* of the house.

JUNE 8, 1865

Billy and the boys have hired a cabin at $10 a month. Slept in the cabin with them last night. Remington[5] played on his guitar during the evening. I lay on the floor in a blanket. The moon cast a clear, soft light over the cabin and in the open doorway, provoking thought & reflection. The music was sad & I grew very very blue and homesick. It came so natural to think of home, friends, and all I so much loved, all lost and far away. I have "no one to love & none to carress." As I write this today I can not help the tears starting. I feel so much alone. Up about

route. Eggs, butter, and flour remained exceedingly scarce. The first regular newspaper mention of eggs available at wholesale prices virtually coincides with Miller's arrival. See *Montana Post*, June 10, 1865. Soon thereafter they dropped in price from ninety to sixty cents a dozen but, by December 2, 1865, rose again to $2.50 a dozen.

4 Several of Virginia City's hotels were named after states of the Union. These included a California Hotel, a Virginia Hotel, a Missouri Hotel, a Wisconsin House, an Idaho Hotel, and a Nebraska House. The *Montana Post* contained advertisements of each.

5 W. H. Remington, popularly known as Mose, was a member of Billy Sheppard's "Troupe of Athletes, Dancers, and Negro Minstrels." The *Montana Post* of June 17, 1865, described him as "a man of vast muscular energy and a scientific Acrobat."

6 o'clock. Ate breakfast, washed a pair of stockings & a handkerchief, blacked my boots & started for the Overland Stage office, the agent having promised to give me an introduction to the firm of Rockfellow & Dennee[6] with whom I hope to get a situation. A few days since I saw Mr. Halsey from Grt. Salt Lake City who gave me an introduction to Mr. Stine & exacted a promise from him to help me get a situation in this city. He introduced me to Messrs. Rockfellow & Dennee. I applied for a situation as a Book Keeper. Mr. Dennee talked favourably but would not give me a definite answer under 3 days time so my chief business will be to wait.

JUNE 9, 1865

Commenced boarding last evening at the Missouri House. Walked to the city, had supper with Billy and the boys. Came back and had supper at the Missouri House, having determined to satisfy my hunger for once at least regardless of consequences.

JUNE 10, 1865

Sick all day, abed most of the time. Sick headache. Bones all aching and very weak. Could not get up to see the boys. Agreed to sell tickets at their exhibition in the theatre tomorrow night.

JUNE 11, 1865

Did not sleep at all last night. Felt slightly better today but very weak. After dinner felt better & walked to the city to attend church, but calling at Billy's cabin first, found they were about to commence the exhibition. As they requested me to take tickets at the door, I spent the evening in the Montana Theatre.[7] Today

6 J. S. Rockfellow, who eventually became territorial treasurer, was one of the leading early citizens of Virginia City. A fellow vigilante, William McK. Dennee, much later became Miller's partner at Deer Lodge, Montana. The original firm of Rockfellow & Dennee, "Wholesale & Retail Grocers, Storage & Commission Merchants," was located at No. 5 Jackson Street, Virginia City. They advertised regularly in the *Montana Post* the sale of such products as glassware, bar fixtures, furniture, and foodstuffs. Rockfellow died in 1868 in Salt Lake City on his way to the East according to memoirs of Bishop D. S. Tuttle. Dennee committed suicide at Spokane in 1890. Virginia City *Madisonian,* November 29, 1890; Deer Lodge *New Northwest,* November 21, 1890.

showed me an entirely new phase of life. There was nothing visible to remind a person in the slightest degree that it was Sunday. Every store, saloon, and dancing hall was in full blast. Hacks running, auctioneering, mining, and indeed every business, is carried on with much more zeal than on week days. It made me heartsick to see it. After the show was over I walked to Nevada at about 12½ o'clock.

JUNE 12, 1865

Slept finely last night. After breakfast walked to Va. City. Saw Mr. Dennee. After talking awhile he told me to call at the store in the afternoon and commence working on his books. Thus after about a week I have secured a situation. Walked to my boarding house for the last time. Very *short* 2 miles *now*. About 3 o'clock walked to the city and called at Rockfellow & Dennee store. Mr. Dennee told me that before seeing me he had promised the situation to another gentleman who was in the office when we had our conversation in the morning. As soon as I left the store he had taken the job away from me. Left the store in very low spirits. Went to an eating saloon to hire myself out at $30 per month but after figuring the matter awhile I concluded I would have enough money after I have sold my eggs to get to San Francisco. Unless I should get a good permanent job to start with, the probabilities are that I would be "Dead-broke" in the spring as expenses "go marching along" in this country, whether profits do or not. Left the restaurant & went to Billy's cabin entirely discouraged. Staid there untill 9 o'clock. Mose [W. H. Remington] played the guitar and sang for a couple of hours. It was fine & soothing. After we walked about the city untill 11 o'clock when I left them & walked to Nevada City. Very dark night & lonely road.

7 The Montana Theatre, which began producing legitimate plays and other attractions as early as 1864, advertised this event in the *Montana Post,* June 10, 1865: "The Keystone Gymnastic Troupe will give a grand exhibition at this well known theatre tomorrow evening June 11th. Billy Sheppard's 'Essence' and little Tommy's contortion are alone worth the price of admission." See also *Montana Post,* June 17, 24, 1865, for glowing accounts of their performances.

JUNE 13, 1865

Up 6 o'clock. After breakfast spent about an hour brushing my overcoat. Then started for Virginia City. Weather cold. Spent the time untill eleven mending my gloves. Walked to Nevada for dinner and [upon returning] resumed mending, this time my overcoat. Staid in a cabin of Mr. Olinghouse[8] untill about 6 o'clock, when I walked "home."

JUNE 14, 1865

Up by 6 o'clock. Not feeling well. Expecting to get a situation I managed to get up. Was disappointed in the job. Lay about 7 hours in the cabin very sick when I succeeded in effecting a negociation for 50 cents. Making my way with much difficulty to the main street, with the assistance of Luke, I took the stage for Nevada City & in due course arrived at the Missouri Hotel. Very sick all the rest of the day. Slept a little at night.

JUNE 15, 1865

Raining all day. Roof of our hotel very leaky. My bed happened to be in a dry corner. Took 5 or 6 powders & 5 pills. Very weak.

JUNE 16, 1865

Rained, snowed, and hailed all day. Horrible weather & very cold. Medicine made me some sicker. Up about noon. Bot some California wine and some Sugar of Lemon. Very good drinks.

JUNE 17, 1865

Up at 7 o'clock. Spent the day sunning myself and reading "Master Humphrey's Clock" by Chas. Dickens.

JUNE 26, 1865

Commenced work for Rockfellow & Dennee. Wages $100 a

8 Messrs. E. Olinghouse & Co. were merchants who owned one of the best stone buildings in Virginia City at the corner of Wallace and Jackson streets. They advertised regularly in the *Montana Post*.

month & board. Board is $72.00 pr. month. Very tiard at night. Worked till 11 o'clock. Duties to keep books of the firm and also to act as clerk.

JULY 7, 1865

News arrived this P.M. of the attack of the stage coach going east while passing thru Port Neuf Kanyon about 180 miles from here on the direct road to Salt Lake City by road agents. Four men killed, one missing and one unhurt. Among the killed was Geo. W. Parker & McCausland.[9] Both were in our store Wednesday, the day the coach left here. Also the missing man Brown[10] was in the office Friday night. The road agents numbered about 20. McCausland was tried for murder a few days ago, having killed a man in Geo. Parker's store. He was acquitted. There is a mass meeting of Vigillantes this evening.

AUGUST 24, 1865

Business dull. My work heavy as usual. After supper took up "Jane Eyre" by Currer Bell.[11] Became very interested in it and read until 2 or 3 o'clock in the morning. It is a well conceived plot, sometimes tending slightly to the coarse in language and idea but intensely interesting. Poor Jane, you have loved as only passionate characters can and after many trials have reached the haven of your desires. The narrative and characters in some instances might almost be substituted for my own—at least the characters with perfect correctness. Mr. Rochester, how I felt the similarity of many points of his character, as drawn, and my own—especially his consuming, maddening love and his sophisticated idea of right and wrong based chiefly on his inclination.

9 This episode is described in Nathaniel Pitt Langford, *Vigilante Days and Ways* (2 vols., Boston, 1890), II, 421–27. See also Thomas J. Dimsdale, *The Vigilantes of Montana* (Norman, 1953), 252. Port Neuf Canyon, through which Miller himself had traveled, was a favorite haunt of highwaymen. It was located about forty miles from Fort Hall, Idaho Territory, and the stage road from Salt Lake City passed through the canyon.

10 Langford, *Vigilante Days*, 425, writes that "Brown escaped by plunging into the surrounding thicket of bushes."

11 The pseudonym of Charlotte Brontë, who first published this book in 1848.

AUGUST 31, 1865

Worked untill late last evening. Mr. Dennee leaving for the States via Salt Lake City.[12] After parting, Mr. Rockfellow retired to the office and wept, like a child, terribly. Beneath a rugged exterior there is sometimes some soft human substance. Sent $257.50 Gold coin by Dennee to Hiller & Snyder, Salt Lake City, to buy some goods. This is the commencement of my first speculation since reaching Va. City.

SEPTEMBER 1, 1865

For 5 hours last evening wrote a copy of "The Montana Ter[ritorial] laws Regulating Elections" without intermission, finishing at one o'clock this morning, for which I received from Col. McLane,[13] the Democratic candidate for Congress, 7th District, $7.00 in gold dust. After dinner while working at my books I discovered a large Grey-back and on examination found my clothes to be thoroughly infested with them. Took a hot bath and bought a new outfit of under-clothes. Sent my clothes to be boiled & washed in salt and water. Commenced raining last evening & rained all day today. Found a fire in the billiard rooms and, after watching the games a bit, found a partner & commenced playing. Played untill 1 o'clock, spending $1.25. On arriving at the store found my blankets missing. I lay upon the counter and nearly froze.

SEPTEMBER 2, 1865

Very unpleasant day. Rained, hailed, and snowed. Mountains white, streets mud a foot deep, air damp-cold and chilly. Trade good. Secured 3 blankets & retired about 8 o'clock.

SEPTEMBER 3, 1865

Weather cold and air damp but rain stopped. Found more

12 As early as August 12, 1865, the *Montana Post* announced dissolution of the partnership of Rockfellow & Dennee. Rockfellow continued in business for himself.
13 Colonel Samuel McLean became the first Montana delegate to Congress. See Tom Stout (ed.), *Montana, Its Story and Biography* (3 vols., Chicago, 1921), I, 207, 218–19, 281–82, 286; Dimsdale, *Vigilantes of Montana*, 59, 63.

Grey-backs on my clothes. Beginning to think I will never get clear of them.

SEPTEMBER 7, 1865

Rain, hail, & snow. Streets muddy and weather chilly. Trade dull. After supper played a couple of games of chess with Mr. ———— and went to bed.

SEPTEMBER 8, 1865

Up about half past 6. About 4 inches of snow on ground & still snowing. No fire in stove. Bought a pair of boots for $12 which, of course, I could only wear a short time.

SEPTEMBER 9, 1865

Up half past six. Snow 3 feet deep and still snowing.

SEPTEMBER 15, 1865

Up ½ past 6 o'clock. Weather fine & pleasant. Trade confined to one sale of $600. After supper walked to top of Burying Ground hill[14] where lie the bodies of what's left of all the road agents hung by the Vigillantes a year or two ago. I enjoyed a good cigar & watched the sun set, a beautifull spectacle away to the west as far as the eye could distinguish. Hill, mountains, and valleys covered with the beauties of Sol's most beautifull colors & beyond, the outlines of still larger, more distant mountains could be traced. Standing cold, grim, & snow clad, bringing me to cold remembrances of past trials and misfortunes, making me not unwillingly turn to thoughts of home. Attended theatre in the evening. "The Two Murderers of France" were tolerably executed. "The Farce of the Lottery Ticket" was well-played. Characters of Wormwood played by G[eorge] Chapman & Susan by Mrs. Flora Caven.[15]

14 Sometimes called Boot Hill Cemetery. Members of the Plummer gang of road agents were later buried there. See Virginia City *Madisonian* (90th Anniversary Edition), May 29, 1953.

15 This performance is described in the *Montana Post*, September 23, 1865. A surprising number of plays and other cultural events were presented at Vir-

SEPTEMBER 17, 1865

Business tolerably dull. Got the blues & attended the theatre in the evening. Play [was] "Six Degrees of Crime." Miserable plot & miserable acting.

SEPTEMBER 20, 1865

Gave $5 toward liquidating the debt of $500 of the Idaho Street Pres. Church in this place.

SEPTEMBER 21, 1865

Up ½ past 6. Dance & supper at the Planter's House last evening.[16] Received a pressing invitation to attend but respectfully declined.

SEPTEMBER 22, 1865

Up a quarter to 7 o'clock. Beautifull weather. The sun shining brightly. Mud returning rapidly to its condition before the rain yesterday. Trade dull. From statement I find the sales for the past 41 days $41,386.93. Evening supper, Raspberries Fresh. Weather growing cold. Prospects of very cold night. Feeling slightly unwell I let my thoughts wander into the old forbidden channell, taking me home to my treasures, my own dear sisters Mary, Emma, & Nettie. Heart sick I have turned to my "Diary" to ease my mind of its load of weary thought, for my poor book is my only friend.

Interrupted and restored to life by a crowd of "Boys" and by having my mind occupied in finding a new washerwoman, my old one having refused to trust me for 25¢.

SEPTEMBER 27, 1865

After being unwell for several days I find myself in very

---

ginia City. About its society Episcopalian Bishop D. S. Tuttle wrote his wife: "Kind hearts are here, cultivated women are here, intelligent society is here." See Tuttle, *Reminiscences*, 131.

16 The Planter's House, the best hotel in Virginia City, was located at the corner of Idaho and Jackson streets. Most stagecoach passengers stayed at this hostelry.

tolerable health this morning. Two men found "hanging in the air" this morning up the gulch a little way with a card on their backs on which were the words "Hung by the Vigilance Committee for being road agents." The bodies were brought into town and placed in a small building where hundreds visited to get a sight of them, myself among the number. Their appearance was anything but prepossessing, with the marks of the rope very visable. Blue faces and open eyes looking very much like when alive.[17]

SEPTEMBER 30, 1865

My dr[ie]d peaches and apples arrived yesterday. I sold them to Mr. Rockfellow at .70¢ & .55¢ respectively. My profits on this speculation are $94.00, making my present capital $2.80 [or $280?] Fine, beautifull summer weather. Recd. a letter from Dan N. He has gone to the States. Entered into speculation No. 2, sending by Mr. Newbanks $305.12 coin to Heller & Snyder.[18]

OCTOBER 7, 1865

Beautifull weather. Up at 6 o'clock. Business dull. Wrote Johnny at St. Joe some days since.

OCTOBER 12, 1865

Received my watch from Salt Lake City through Mr. Bruce in good order. After storming two or three days it cleared off yesterday. Weather fine outdoors today but damp and unhealthy indoors. Sorted peaches untill 8½ o'clock and retired.

OCTOBER 15, 1865

Trade good. Weather fine. After supper I concluded to attend church and started for the Sanctum Meeting. Joe Dow-

17 Although vigilante activity at Virginia City had diminished in 1865, occasional punishments of this sort were still meted out. See *Montana Post*, September 30, 1865, for a description of the hangings to which Miller refers.

18 Miller's previous commercial contacts at Salt Lake City were now of considerable help to him. Fortunately Rockfellow, who became a close personal friend, allowed him to carry on various "speculations," such as the importing of produce, eggs, salt, and matches.

delohe persuaded me to visit Capt. Rogers.[19] Found Queen and her two sisters at home. After remaining about an hour proceeded to the church after which we visited the dance houses. Played a game of billiards and retired. Much merriment, caused by our efforts to sleep both of us in my single bed, brought to a close by Joe sleeping with Rockfellow.

OCTOBER 17, 1865

Invitation to ball at Planter's [House]. Concluded to go and purchased suit of clothes to go in.

Coat $35
Pants & vest $43.50
Hat $13
Shirt 4.50
Kneckerchief 1.75
Hdkerchief $1.50
Gaiters $6.00
_____

$105.25

After arranging my toilet I awaited the opening of the dance until 10 o'clock. The music not having arrived, I and some others, having used the fire water rather freely, felt the effects so much that I changed my mind and concluded not to go & went to bed accordingly.

OCTOBER 18, 1865

Sold the balance of my peaches for 20¢, 216 [lbs.?], they being full of worms and good for nothing. Owing to this reason my first speculation is a losing one to the tune of $20.

OCTOBER 20, 1865

Was offered a situation by Higgins & Haggadorn[20] $100 a

19 Possibly W. H. Rodgers, proprietor of the Missouri House, where Miller lived. See Michael Leeson (ed.), *History of Montana* (Chicago, 1885), 1316.

20 Francis G. Higgins became a prominent citizen of Montana who later gave land for the present site of the University of Montana. See Stout, *Montana Story*, I, 532.

month and Board. Not wishing to accept, I walked to Nevada City in search of Mr. Morrison who I knew to be out of employment and who was clerk at Ray's Missouri House when I boarded there. Could not find him, however, and I returned, my pocket lightened $2.00 by the trip. Had quite a long conversation in the evening with Mr. Smith, the Presbyterian minister whose life, as he told it to me, recalled my almost forgotten resolve to save every penny of my money untill I acquired sufficient to take me through College.

OCTOBER 21, 1865

Business very dull. Beautifull weather. After supper played 4 games of Billiards with Capt. Maltby winning. Victorious in 2 of the 4.

OCTOBER 22, 1865

Recd circular from Princeton College of New Jersey by which I find that the amount necessary to go through College in good style is $2000.

Resolved:
That from this date I do not spend a cent for foolish expenses such as Billiards, Drinking or Eating, Driving, Riding, Smoking, that I limit my monthly expenses for Dancing & Gifts to $10.00.

OCTOBER 23, 1865

Change of the weather during the night. Morning cold wind with slight quantity of snow falling. Same weather all day. Growing colder untill night. Could not write on the books, it being so cold and we having no stove. Resolution intact.

OCTOBER 24, 1865

Cold during the night, preventing sleep. Up at 7 o'clock. About 3 inches of snow had fallen during the night. Bought a 5 gal. keg beer, which I propose to drink for my health. Cost 2.00

pr. gal. Weather cold but pleasant. Wrote untill 9 o'clock getting accounts ready for Rockfellow who goes to Helena in the morning to officiate as Pemberton's right hand.[21] Resolution intact.

NOVEMBER 3, 1865

Business dull. Weather very warm and pleasant but muddy. After supper I resumed "Les Miserables" by Victor Hugo. Becoming interested I read untill 3 o'clock in the morning. It is a fine plot, as good as "Never Was." Two qualities it possesses do not suit me, however. One is the almost vulgar comments & passages about virtue etc., another the fallacies so thickly spread through it and the "Frenchy" ideas concerning progress, religion, etc. Resolution broken & reformed.

NOVEMBER 4, 1865

Played a game of chess & was "punished" terribly. Resolution intact.

NOVEMBER 7, 1865

After supper I and Captain Maltby[22] played 4 games of billiards, I beat him twice after which we bowled 11 games in the Bowling saloon. Resolution broken.

NOVEMBER 8, 1865

Played 7 games billiards & bowled 3 games with Capt. Maltby. Beat 2 billiards & 2 bowls.

NOVEMBER 9, 1865

Beautifull morning, warm, shiney day. Snow has disappeared

21 Rockfellow was the best man at the wedding of William T. Pemberton, an early pioneer who moved to Helena from Virginia City in 1865. See Stout, *Montana Story*, I, 435; the *Montana Post*, October 28, 1865, stated that he had "immolated himself on the altar of Hymen. Delightful sacrifice!"

22 Possibly this is the Maltby mentioned in Leeson, *History of Montana*, 170. The *Montana Post* for November 25, 1865, mentions the arrest of W. H. Maltby for engaging in a "confidence game." A Captain W. J. Maltby, later a Texas Ranger, wrote a book about his experiences in the West entitled *Captain Jeff . . .* (Colorado, Texas, 1906).

& roads unobstructed. Resolution formed with firm determination to keep it.

NOVEMBER 10, 1865

Peaches arrived from Salt Lake today. 830 lbs. Sold them at 60¢. Profits on this Spec[ulation] No. 2 was $90.00. My present capital is $175.00. Borrowed Do. $100.00 making $275.00 which I have invested in matches which is Speculation No. 3. Cost of matches from $5.20 to $9.00 pr. case of 2 doz. small boxes. Spent during the Month of October for clothes & frolic $195.12. Have received since reaching this city:

Salary	$400
Brought	$100
Horse & saddle	$ 70
	$570
(on hand $175.00)	
(Lost Spec. No. 1, $25.00)	$200
	$370
Profit Spec. No. 2 & 3 (90 & 40)	$120
Spent in 4 months	$500*
Doctor's Bill	$ 20
	$480

* Miller's arithmetic is in error.

NOVEMBER 13, 1865

Weather cloudy, a little rain. Read "Shirley" until 2 o'clock A.M. last eve, a finely written piece inferior in plot to "Jane Eyre" but much superior in description and language. Intended going to church but Fairfield, wishing to make a call, I gave it up and spent the evening in the store. Rockey back from Hot Springs where he has been four or five days. Streets terrible muddy. Started my "cabinet" with a Black flint arrow, 3 moss agates & a piece of petrified wood. The agates come from lower Utah Ter [ritory] though similar ores are found in the vicinity of the Jefferson & Stinking Water streams. Weighed myself today, 144 lbs. against 131 lbs. which was my weight when I reached my Birthday.

NOVEMBER 14, 1865

Rained hard last night. Very muddy today.

NOVEMBER 15, 1865

Read "Harper's" untill 12 o'clock last evening. Snowed all night. About 3 inches of snow and three of mud offer their inducements to the pedestrian.

NOVEMBER 16, 1865

Pursuant to a printed circular issued & signed by Jno. H. Ming, Ben Dittes, & Jno. S. Rockfellow committee a number of young men, myself among the number, and 13 in all, met at John Ming's store and organized, or rather took the initiatory steps to organize the "Va. City Social Club." After appointing a committee on Rooms and one on "Principals, Laws, and Regulations," we adjourned to meet Saturday at the County Recorder's office.[23]

NOVEMBER 17, 1865

Played a number of Billiards with Capt. Maltby & drank an immense quantity of Tom & Jerry, about 13 glasses of spirits "much elevated." Sick during the night. Very muddy.

[23] This is the first recorded account of the existence of such a cultural organization. The *Montana Post* for November 18, 1865, hailed its founding. Ben R. Dittes, who owned the first printing press in Montana, became a co-owner of the *Montana Post* and, in 1868, Helena's first librarian. See Roby Wentz, *Eleven Western Presses* (Los Angeles, 1956), 49–51. See Stout, *Montana Story*, I, 757, 760. John H. Ming, a prominent merchant, stocked books as well as groceries, shoes, and stationery at his store on the corner of Wallace and Jackson streets. Above Rockfellow's store Ming also operated the Occidental Billiard Hall. He advertised regularly in the *Montana Post* and eventually became territorial auditor.

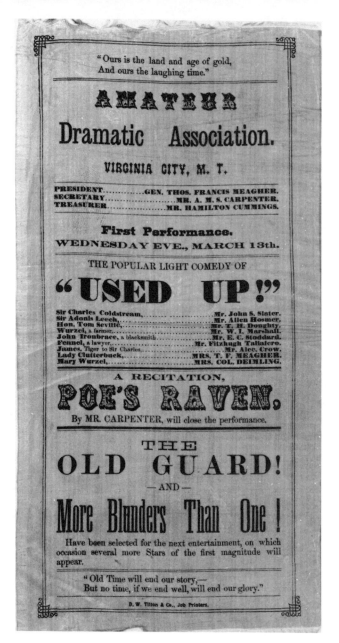

Program of amateur theatricals printed on silk and illustrative of the numerous performances attended by Miller in Virginia City. Miller made reference to the unusual variety of such dramatic activities in early Montana.

The dramatic group to which Miller belonged (1866). Miller is third from left (front row), with mustache.

NOVEMBER 18, 1865

Terrible wind & rain storm. Meeting very well attended. Laws adopted. Myself and Hill added to the committee on laws.

NOVEMBER 23, 1865

Commenced snowing about 10 o'clock A.M. continued snowing a couple of hours. Afternoon weather cold. After tea about 10 o'clock I and the doctor endeavored to discover the comet but without success. Flour up $1 per sack, retailing at $25 pr. 100 sack.

NOVEMBER 24, 1865

Up 7 o'clock. Weather cold & bracing, a thin coat of snow covering the mountains around. Secured three members for the Society. Had many serious thoughts tonight of home and suffered severely from a conflict between my resolve of last New Year never to communicate with any of my friends untill with money to back me and my longing to write Mary [Miller] & hear the news. I so long to hear from her. The result of the conflict was in favour of my resolution, my first step toward making a fortune having been taken, that is submission to the will of others when in order to further the end I have in view. I will, God willing and assisting me, persevere to the end. Coming a stranger into a strange land I have today $500 in cash, a pure situation untill the spring, a kind employer, many friends, and not a single enemy that I know of, not having done a single dishonest action since August the 10th, 1864. I have certainly taken a step towards my object. For the last time I make the following resolves:

> To limit my expenses for Billiards, Drinking, Eating, driving, riding, smoking and dancing to $10 pr. month. The first of each month to record my success & the "day of the evil" my failure in keeping my resolve.

NOVEMBER 27, 1865

Commenced boarding at Mrs. Thwing's. Johnny Keefer off for Salt Lake. He proposes to invest $4,500 which he has with him in goods & teams & bring them to this place. Sent by him $100 and am to have 1/450 part of the profit. This is Speculation No. 4. Fine weather. This evening drew up twenty standing resolutions for the government of our club. Wrote untill 11½ o'clock.

NOVEMBER 28, 1865

Meeting in the evening. Collected 8 men to the meeting, 4 of whom signed as members. Had full meeting of 22 members present. Passed 20 standing resolutions. There are now 25 members to the association.

NOVEMBER 29, 1865

Reports in circulation of the robbery of the coach that Keefer left in but no apparent foundation for them.

NOVEMBER 30, 1865

Morning snowing slowly. It stopped snowing at 11 o'clock. Commenced again at three. Still snowing at 10 o'clock. Finished Wilkie Collins' "Views afoot in Cornwall County, England."[24]

DECEMBER 2, 1865

At daylight thermometer at zero. During the day a cold north wind. Absence of any heat from the sun and the drifting & falling snow made it decidedly unpleasant out of doors. A couple of Missourians, 6-footers, started across the range for Hot Springs but concluded to return. A few cases of frozen noses & ears heard of.

DECEMBER 3, 1865

Breakfasted at 9:20 o'clock, Mrs. Thwing having "slept over"

24 *Rambles Beyond Railways*, or *Notes in Cornwall Taken Afoot* (London, 1851).

herself. Had a discussion with Dr. Justice at the table regarding the elements of a "Yankee," he contending that they were not "fit to live." Was utterly disgusted at his narrow, vain, conceited ideas of a northern man. They are a fair sample of those of a majority of the secessionists as far as I have known them.[25] Thermometer at zero this morning. Very cold last night. Water frozen in store. Very little trade.

DECEMBER 4, 1865

Clear cold winter weather. After supper started to play a game of billiards with Jno. Ming. After playing one game and being beaten I and David Haggadorn played untill 3 o'clock in the morning. The opposition, Thos. Hoopes & another gent., beat us & I beat Haggadorn, giving him 40 points & beating him 30 points. Drank an enormous quantity of beer but with no ill effects.

DECEMBER 5, 1865

Poor health all day. Evening Association met at our store. I was elected Corresponding Secretary. Adjourned to meet in our hall. 12 members present.

DECEMBER 8, 1865

In the morning completed my arrangements for the sleighride to be by the Y. M. Literary Association to the Amphion Serenaders at 6:20 o'clock. Jas. Thompson and myself accompanied by Smith, Pres[d]t. of the Association. Proceeded to the Room of the Amphions. Delivered our testimonial of thanks for their offer to our Association of their musical services, for one benefit. Also delivered an invitation signed by the Pres[d]t. & Secty. of our Association inviting them to enjoy a sleigh-ride. The invitation being accepted, we left the Amphion finding the sleigh & robes ready to start. I had some difficulty in persuading

25 A number of Southern sympathizers were in Virginia City at this time. Earlier they had attempted to name the town Varina after the wife of Jefferson Davis. Some of these persons came west to escape military service. Others were deserters.

Rocky & Colonel [F. C.] Deimling to go but finally they allowed all my designs & started again for the room of the Amphion. Arriving at the place we received 10 Amphions into the sleigh & started on our ride. Very crowded sleigh, about 18 inside. Rode through all the streets & to Nevada City & back. Took possession of several saloons, among them Mings, the bowling saloon, Rockey Thomas'. Had a *carousing* time generally & most of us got two thirds "Over the bay." Finally those left of us about 8 adjourned to the chap house for an Oyster Supper. Then I left the crowd and retired to bed.

DECEMBER 9, 1865

Took $60 in greenbacks this morning & started to pay my bills of last night. When through had $15 left. Cost $45 & $10 spent last night. Total cost $55. All those in our crowd last night were today summoned to appear before Judge Tal[l]iaferro in the Police Court at three o'clock P.M.[26] There were 27 of us. Our first action in the premises was to march in a crowd to the offices of every lawyer in the City and secure their services as counsel. At three o'clock we all assembled in the court and were argued upon by Ward Strickland[27] for the defence & Wm. H. Chiles for the prosecution. After several attempts without success of our counsel to obtain a change of venue the court adjourned untill 6 o'clock, when we will be tried by a jury of six. Court in session at six & trial proceeded after hearing the testimony of the prosecuting witnesses during which the old blue laws of Connecticut were read. The jury retired, remained about 10 minutes & returned a verdict of not-guilty. This was on Jim Thompson's case, it having been determined to try each one seperately. After the verdict the City Attorney[28] made a few remarks & said he

26 The Amphion Serenaders had previously gotten into trouble for their carousing. The *Montana Post,* December 16, 1865, called them the "wicked serenaders." Judge T. W. Talliaferro was police magistrate of Virginia City.

27 O. F. Strickland was one of a group of Virginia City's first lawyers.

28 William Chumasero, whose daughter Miller later married, became a well-known Montana Judge. At Virginia City he also carried on a private practice, and his office was located in J. H. Ming's store, corner of Wallace and Jackson streets. See *Montana Post,* September 17, 1864.

would enter a Noles Prosequi in the other cases. The judge thereupon did and so, duly discharged, we all adjourned to take a drink. Serenaded the Governor, then adjourned to Rocky Thomas' Saloon where I left them & retired.

DECEMBER 19, 1865

Attended the Inauguration Ball of the Literary Society. It was a decided success, there being 25 couples present. Dedication speech by Prof. Dimsdale[29] after which the time was occupied with dancing and supper untill 3 A.M. I made my "debut" dancing the first time with Mrs. Lovell, afterwards with [Fanny] Lovell, Jennie Lovell, Mrs. Lovell,[30] Puss Ray, Miss Boice Jr., & Mrs. Castner. Made lots of blunders but steadily improved. Splendid supper, fine music, good floor & sleigh & food.

DECEMBER 25, 1865

Last evening partook of milk punch at Ben Wood's. Geo. Hill, Geo. Heldt, Jas. Thompson, Jas. McShane, Jno. Ming, John Rockfellow were also there. Worked on the books untill noon. Everybody on a spree. Store closed. Spent the day very quietly. Played 3 games of billiards in the afternoon. Read a novel during the evening. Had a very poor Christmas dinner of beef. Made one present to little Mary Piles.

[29] "Professor" Thomas J. Dimsdale, an Englishman, was the editor of the *Montana Post,* Virginia City's first newspaper. He wrote a series of articles about vigilanteism later republished as *The Vigilantes of Montana* (Great Falls, 1866; Norman, 1953), probably the first book published in Montana. This volume, of which five editions exist, gives the earliest printed view of the maintenance of justice and the lawless conditions in the mining camps of the Rocky Mountains. Dimsdale also organized the first school at Virginia City, a short-lived venture. A recollection by one of his students is in Margaret Ronan (ed.), "Memoirs of a Frontiers Woman, Mary C. Ronan" (M. A. thesis, University of Montana, 1932), 52–55. See also *Montana Post,* September 17, 1864, and December 3, 1864. The dedication of the literary society's hall is described in the December 16 and 23, 1865, issues of the newspaper.

[30] The wife of W. L. Lovell, an early Virginia City attorney and later judge. Both played a prominent part in starting the first Episcopal church in Montana. See Tuttle, *Reminiscences,* 118–44, concerning religion in early Montana.

JANUARY 1, 1866

New Years! Morning beautiful weather. Clear, calm and pleasant, with enough snow on the ground to make splendid sleighing[31] and cold enough to enjoy the comfort of an overcoat. Up and at work on the books at 8 A.M. Store closed. Had considerable difficulty in deciding whether I would make New Years calls or not. Somebody asking me if I were going to the Prize-fight, decided the matter and at 12 I proceeded to Nelson's Hall having ticketed myself for $5.00. A very rough looking crowd duly assembled consisting in great proportion of Irish, a sprinkling of Dutch and a smaller number of gents. After waiting for 2 hours for the fight and at the same time a snow storm commenced and thirty rounds were fought. The result was a decided victory for Con.[32] Patsey Marley, his antagonist, being dreadfully punished, having both eyes closed, his nose & face bruised & mashed to a jelly. Shouted myself hoarse hurrahing for Con from "Principle," he being an acquaintance of mine. This is the first prize fight I ever attended. At the commencement I felt a disgust that almost destroyed all the interest I took in the fight. As the fight

31 Sleighing became a favorite outdoor sport in early Virginia City. The *Montana Post* for December 30, 1865, stated: "Among the latest and most original outfits, a man might have been seen on horse-back, dragging a rude hand-sleigh. . . . Both sexes and all ages have, apparently, determined upon getting all the amusement possible out of the snow and holidays." Sleighing parties were sometimes followed by "oyster suppers." Aside from Rockfellow, Miller went sleighing and serenading with young men who later became prominent in Montana: F. George Heldt was a merchant at Great Falls; *Register, Society of Montana Pioneers* (2 vols., Akron, 1899), I, 64–65. George Hill became one of the founders of North Hill in Choteau County, Montana; see Leeson, *History of Montana*, 509. James McShane was a member of the first city council of Virginia City; see *ibid.*, 774. James Thompson became under sheriff of Missoula County; see *ibid.*, 871.

32 J. C. "Con" Orem gave private boxing lessons at the Champion Saloon and was the most renowned pugilist in early Montana. On January 3, 1865 (unpublished diary of James Henry Morley, Montana Historical Society) Orem fought a 193-round fight with Hugh O'Neil. His best opposition came from Patsey Marley, a New York pug. On November 11, 1865, they fought over ninety rounds near Helena, a contest attended by 2,500 people which ended only by the coming of darkness. Their New Year's Day, 1865, engagement, fought in Leviathan Hall, Virginia City, was ninety-nine rounds long. After the ninety-fourth round, Marley "fell under the ropes and struck his forehead on a log," according to the *Montana Post,* January 6, 1866. Regarding Orem, Tuttle, and other Virginia City pioneers mentioned by Miller, see A. K. McClure, *Three Thousand Miles Through the Rocky Mountains* (Philadelphia, 1869), 338–41, 384–85.

progressed, however, all such feelings speedily vanished and the excitement which followed made the fight both interesting and enjoyable. After the fight, returned to the Occidental Billiard Hall & played Jno. Ming a game for the Oyster Dinners, the result being in my favor. After dinner at the Star [Restaurant] returned to the Occidental & played Jno. Ming three games all in my favor. Tom Hoopes 5 games lost from the Capt. 6 games lost 5. The Capt. lost the supper & eating a "stew"[33] we retired & thus ended my first New Years spent in Montana.

JANUARY 3, 1866

Rockey discharged Fairfield tonight of suspicion of dishonesty. Very glad he has left as I did not like him. Called on Mrs. Piles in the evening. Society meeting to-night.

JANUARY 7, 1866

Store closed to-day first Sunday. Attended Episcopal services in the morning. Methodist Sunday School at 2 P.M. & intended attending Presbyterian Meeting at night but, happening to be in the Occidental, I was unable to resist the temptation & played 11 games losing about $20.00 in games & drinks. Was reelected Corresponding Secty. of the Young Men's Literary Association last meeting.

JANUARY 9, 1866

Attended & took active part in meeting to-night. Was appointed one of a committee of 4 to draw up a plan for carrying on the Literary pursuits of the Association. Col. Deimling[34] Mr. Gillette & Prof. Dimsdale being my fellow committee men. Was also empowered to collect & have control of all newspapers belonging to the Association.

---

33 Thomas Hoopes, who was playing with "the Capt.," became a wholesale merchant at both Virginia City and Helena. He died in 1881. Helena *Weekly Herald,* January 6, 1881.

34 Colonel F. C. Deimling, admitted to the Montana bar in 1868, was the recording secretary of the Mining Bureau of Montana and also secretary of the Union party in Montana. *Montana Post,* April 7, 1866, and Leeson, *History of Montana,* 321. His name is often misspelled, as it is in Helen F. Sanders and William H. Bertsche, Jr. (eds.), *X. Beidler: Vigilante* (Norman, 1957), 130, an account by the widely known Montana sheriff.

FEBRUARY 20, 1866

Evening meeting at Y. M. L. A. Only 7 men were present. Finished "David Copperfield" [by] Chas. Dickens, sitting up untill the "wee small hours of the morning." Was very interested in the book. The plot is fine, the language irreproachable. The conception of characters very truthfull and the description insurpassable. How beautifull Mr. Peggotty's character & how sweet Dora's, the child wife. "Though my dear boy is so lonely before his child-wife's empty chair." "Oh how my poor boy cries! hush, Hush! xxxxxx "It is much better as it is." What a perfect picture he draws of a Pure Innocent loving Dear Child-wife. Too fair, too fragile, breaking her heart at an unkind word. A beautifull creation. Almost too beautifull to be read.

At about 8 o'clock Capt. Maltby attracted my attention to a beautifull display of the "Aurore Boraealis" or Northern Lights the most beautifull I had ever beheld. About 1/5 of the heavens was of a dark fiery red color forming a shape of a band of red around the horizon, numerous shafts of soft white color running perpendicularly divided the red into as many different parts and one broad band of light at the right of north. Constantly changing from one position to another sometimes shining bright making the earth light, in an instant shifting to another place. It seemed to be the advance guard of the main body which comparatively stationary showed a steady beautifull spectacle of red & white streaks. Rockfellow and a lot of the "Boys" on a terrible spree. Not in the house untill 5:20 o'clock.

FEBRUARY 21, 1866

Commenced a steady blowing drifting snow storm compelling a person to limit his observation to a few yards distance. Evening not snowing. Attended the opening of the "New Peoples Theatre"[35] which was today completed. Very cold enjoyment. Play "The Hunchback," the only stove in the building

---

[35] This venture was begun early in 1866. "The Hunchback" was the theater's initial performance. It was reviewed in the *Montana Post,* February 24, 1866.

not affecting seemingly anyone with any particle of warmth. After freezing through the first play Capt. Maltby & myself proceeded to Occidental Billiard Hall.

At 4 o'clock A.M. I quit the "Amusement" the loser of 20 games & drinks. $10 total loss.

FEBRUARY 22, 1866

Bracing winter weather, clear & cold with warm sun shining. Feel rather tired from effects of last night.

MARCH 1, 1866

Statement of assets & liabilities

> Assets, Cash sent to Salt Lake, $270
> Due Harry $115
>   ″   Johnny $50
>   ″   Rockey $40
>   ─────
> $205
>
> $65 present capital

MARCH 14, 1866

Attended Miss Annie Boice to the theatre. Play "The Marble Heart." Miss Boice very pleasant lady but not a very able conversationist and hardly old enough to be a "young" lady. In fact, I found it, as I always do, a "task" rather than a pleasure to entertain a silent lady or rather one not *very talkative*. The plot of the "Marble Heart" did not suit me. The seat I had was a poor one. My toes were cold and my temper hot and altogether I determined that I had quite enough of that. Miss Boice a very *nice* young lady, as the saying goes.

MARCH 15, 1866

About a week since a meeting was held for the purpose of

organizing a third House (mock) to sit with the Legislature now in session in the city. Last meeting I did not attend. Being advised that I was to be reported a member from ———, I presented myself at about 8 P.M. Meeting being called to order and roll called, the house proceeded to business. Harry (our darkey) occupied a desk having the label "Territorial Reporter" attached to the front part in view of the audience, a marking pot & brush, and some very goodly sized brown wrapping paper represented respectively ink, pen and paper. A platform three feet or more high had been erected on which the chair for the "Page" was placed. Dick Berry a gentleman about six feet three occupied the chair having been elected at the previous meeting. The speaker's mace, a log about a foot in diameter and three feet long tapering towards the top untill of right size to hold in the hand, occupied a prominent position on the table. Motion made to appoint a committee of sixteen to wait upon the Governor and "Inform his excellency the House was fully organized and awaited any communication he may choose to make" was carried. A motion to amend by appointing a committee of three, including the Territorial Reporter, to wait upon the Governor and with a wheelbarrow convey him hither. Ayes 71. Noes 6. Motion lost. After an interval of a few seconds the Governor appeared and amid loud and long continued applause commenced the delivery of his message, a very able document, the main point being a donation of two million dollars to the territory of Misselaneum. At the conclusion a motion to print two million seven hundred thousand copies was lost. Various reports were held & the committee of Means & Ways, Rockfellow chairman at their request, was continued, also the committee on Wet Stationary and others. Various motions & resolutions and notices were read by the clerk and at ten o'clock the meeting adjourned. Much fun was made. Finished "Kenilworth" by Sir Walter Scott, a novel of tolerable merits. Very beautiful weather.

JUNE 5, 1866

Wagered Mr. Rockfellow a new hat, the best to be had in the

territory, that within one year from this date flour would not be sold at over $15.00 per sack in lots of 100 sacks or more.

JUNE 7, 1866

The day was commenced or inaugurated with a damp cold rain lasting a couple of hours followed by a hail storm after which came snow quite lively and heavy for an hour or two. After this, treating us to a complete assortment of weather, old [Sol?] went back to first principles, a steady rain for the balance of the day and evening. Cold, wet, and dreary.

Geo. and I having sent Mrs. Ben Wood a couple pounds of sugar this P.M. for the purpose of making some candy, presented ourselves at the house to conclude the experiment with our "Masticators" prepared. A very pleasant evening "pulling" candy.

JUNE 8, 1866

I ate so much candy last evening that I neither gained any in sleep during the night nor good looks this morning. Vowing candy a "bore," I have resolved to "shun" it for the future. Another snow storm today. Delightful weather in June. Trade is nearly played out here. Virginia looks like a large town minus the people. Mr. Rockfellow gone to Hot Spring District. I am "grand manager" and have entire controll during Mr. Rockfellow's absence. We had a grand Base Ball match Sunday before last. I append an account of the same cut from the "Post." I am Secretary of the Organization. My financial condition just at the present time is bad—decidedly bad. Some time ago I sent to Heller & Snyder $40 to invest and ship to me. $240 borrowed, or rather sent, for another man by my recommendation to buy some stationary (Mr. Ming) as he went by my advice and is a friend of mine I feel bound to secure him against loss. Messrs. H[eller] & S[nyder] having had the bad grace to fail, I sent the account to Jimmy Brown at Salt Lake City to collect. Thus far he has recovered $15 in cash and about $125 in goods. On the balance there are many possibilities of my losing. As near as possible I now stand, monetarilly speaking, as follows:

Due Harry	$125		Due from Helena	$125
" Ming	$200		" " Salt Lake	$275
" J.S.R.	$ 65			$400
" Jno. Keefer	$ 15			
	$405			
	$400			
	$5			

$5 worse off than nothing after a year's work in such a country as this. $3500 worse off than when I left the states. I much doubt whether the Lord ever intends to let me make another "Pile." However a "stiff upper lip" was always my characteristic and it does not fail me now.

JUNE 15, 1866

Purchased 4760# of salt at 8¢ per lb. on speculation. Stored it in Mr. Rockfellow's cellar. Borrowed $375 of Jas. Clasby at 5% per mo. giving him as collateral my watch and a receipt for the Salt Lake goods.

JULY 18, 1866

About a month since I purchased 4758# salt @ 8¢ per lb. It has since advanced and I am very sure of getting 15¢ for it. The following is my Monetary condition today

Due J. S. R[ockfellow]	6.06	Due from Jno Wickell	$23.90
" Jas Clasby	154.70	" Gross Mchs.	
" J. H. M[ing]	129.50	@ $20	$80.00
" Harry	100.	5930# salt	$889.50
" [Johnny] Keefer	5		$993.40
" on salt	40		$435.26
	$435.26		558.14

Which makes my present worth $558.14, a gain of $563.14 since

June 8 a very good profit considering that my salary is only $125 per month.

JUNE 19, 1866

Attended the theatre last evening. Saw Julia Dean Hayne Cooper in Grisaldis as "Grisaldis."[36] She is a fine actress, a fine figure though not very strikingly handsome. I recd. an introduction to her by Mr. Cooper who is escorting her through the country intending to go down the river to St. Louis whence she will go to N. Y. & meet her husband from New York. A recruiting trip to Europe is anticipated. Mr. Cooper (the one here), with whom I had become about as intimately acquainted as I usually do with anyone, is a well educated brilliant young man. His contributions to "Harper's Monthly" are numerous and varied, embracing both Poetry & Prose articles. His signature is "N. Y. Shepherd"

JULY 27, 1866

Mr. Rockfellow having returned from Benton, where he has been for a couple of weeks attending to the shipment of goods for the store, I notified him that unless my salary was increased to $150 per month, and with board, I could no longer remain with him as Mr. Hussey [?] Bunker had so offered me. He hesitated but after a while acceeded to my request & I today *rented* myself to him for one year at $150 & board per month, equal to about $2500 per year. The privilege of speculating is also included in the agreement.

DECEMBER 25, 1866

Merry Christmas for the second time in Montana. Would hardly have known or been aware of its approach, were it not for the effect it has had on Mr. Hammel, who is teaching me French. He has been somewhat irregular in the delivery of instructions, owing to his endeavors to be a "shining light" in the Catholic choir of this city during the Christmas festivities.

[36] The *Montana Post*, July 21, 1866, reported this play as "Leah, the Forsaken." It was performed in the People's Theatre.

Christmas morning weather fine, clear and bracing, the air almost seeming to contain the elixir of life so pure and exhilarating. Store not closed, business dull. After dining on substitute turkey, with wine for salad, I graciously accepted Mr. Rockfellow's invitation to join him with my company for a sleigh ride and "behind the prancing steeds merrily we rode" with only one tip over & two cigars apiece. After the ride I returned to my position as a counter jumper and after several ineffectual attempts to seduce some men to buy "goods", I supped on victuals and studied French for a couple of hours & spent the balance of the night with morphius.

JANUARY 18, 1867

Mr. Rockfellow at Bannack. I spent the day in doing literally nothing at all. No trade, no calls, nothing to show that 1867 was among the things that were. Weather clear and bracing, a beautiful day and only one of an almost countless number that we have been favored with in this dreaded and shivered-at locality.

Another year has gone and brought some few changes to me. At the commencement of the year my salary was $100 per month and board. Now I am receiving $175 per month and board which is $16.00 per week or $64.00 more, which is equal to $2848 per year in gold. Treasury notes can be purchased here at 85¢ which makes my present salary about $3350 in total. Quite a liberal allowance. On the 8th of June last about 7 mos. ago I was in debt $5.00. Now I have $1197 capital. On or about the first of May next I am going to start from here for Paris and the continent mainly to be present at the French Exposition Universal. My expenses will be paid from here to the States by parties for whom I will carry treasure and I fully expect to be able to muster $2000 when I get there in gold coin. Just now I am studying French with Mr. Hammel in order to facilitate my acquisition of the French language when I reach Paris. I have not heard from a relation and know nothing whatever of the changes at home.

JANUARY 27, 1867

Attended the lecture of Thos. Francis Meagher given at the rooms of the House of Rep. of the Territory for the benefit of the "funds & charities of the Catholic church with Mr. Ed Calhoun as my "protege." His subject was "The Irish Brigade & the army of the Potomac." Very ably treated by the Gen. As the general is upon his "Hunting grounds" when treating upon the Irish, he was most elequent, his discourse abounding in pathos & continually convulsing his audience with laughter & anon receiving long and continued applause for a brilliant rhetorical effort. As a historical effort it was almost valueless but to the lover of beautiful description & "live" language it was a decided treat. The hall was densely packed, the audience coming near to the "stack" order.[37]

JANUARY 29, 1867

"The" wedding of the territory came off tonight. My employer Mr. R[ockfellow] has for the last two months been occupied in building and furnishing a house, having "sinnister" intentions regarding the same. Tonight the climax was capped and Rocky demitted from the Batchellor club. The ceremony took place at Mr. Lovell's[38] at about 8 o'clock. The bride, Miss Mollie McNiel, was very beautifull, the very picture of self possessed purity. The room was very small, the bride very little, and the ceremony very short. After the ceremony salutes and congratulations were given to the couple and they were immediately transferred by wagon to the mansion on the hill.[39] Some time afterwards, about half an hour, I gained admission into the vehicle and in due course of time arrived at the house. About

---

[37] The colorful General Thomas Francis Meagher was first secretary of Montana Territory and in 1865 acting governor. A native of Ireland, he raised an Irish regiment during the Civil War with which he fought with distinction. See Robert G. Athearn, *Thomas Francis Meagher: An Irish Revolutionary in America* (Boulder, 1949).

[38] W. Y. Lovell became probate judge of Madison County, Montana Territory.

[39] This home, by far the best in Virginia City, was still standing in 1957. A description of it appeared in the *Montana Post*, February 2, 1867: "It is decidedly superior to any other dwelling in the Territory."

nine o'clock the company commenced arriving and one continued stream of mud, snow, silks, beauty & humanity poured in upon us. The crowd duly separated Harry, Geo. R., & myself. At about 10 o'clock supper commenced and continued without intermission for three hours. The "affair" was a positive success got up regardless of expense and the company assembled comprised the elite of the country, among them the always prominent Mrs. Genl. Meagher, a very good representative of the grand lady, a superb lady. Very much like an immense work. She is very good to be seen at the proper distance but too large and unwieldy for a life companion. I am only slightly acquainted with her but from others I hear that she is a highly educated, versatile, and very agreeable lady. A "grin" among acquaintances.[40]

MARCH 10, 1867

Dined at Mr. Rockfellow's. I have only missed one Sunday dinner (last) since his marriage. Attended Sunday School for the first time in 11 months. Took a dose of French (lesson) with Capt. DeLacy.[41]

MARCH 11, 1867

Last evening we (the inhabitants) were treated to a meteor, a luminous body travelling seemingly at a not very great elevation in a southeasterly direction. Two seperate explosions took place throwing particles and being distinctly heard. The flash lit up the heavens like the sun at noonday and everybody rushed for the street, thinking a fire had broken out. Weather very cold and disagreeable. Thermometer below zero all day and 12° at 6 o'clock P.M.

40 Mrs. Meagher, corpulent wife of the acting territorial governor, was a favorite Virginia City hostess. See Tuttle, *Reminiscences,* 135.

41 Colonel W. W. De Lacy, a Virginian, was a West Point graduate, a former United States Navy officer, a significant explorer, and a teacher of languages. He was a surveyor and map maker of note and official photographer for the first Montana Territorial Legislature. See Frank Harmon Garver, "First Official Map of Montana Territory," Butte *Post,* December 24, 1915. See Stout, *Montana Story,* I, 200–201.

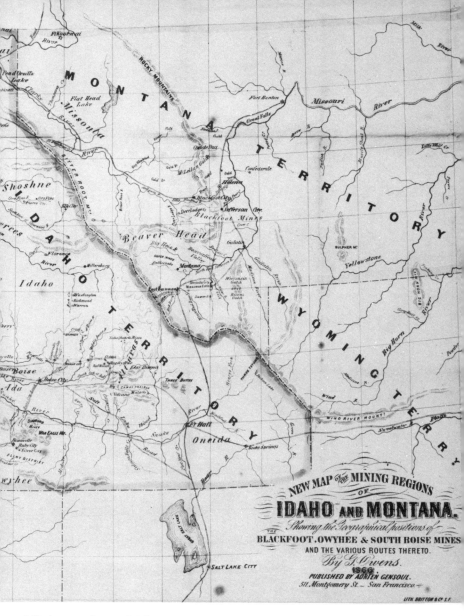

Mining regions of Idaho and Montana, 1866.

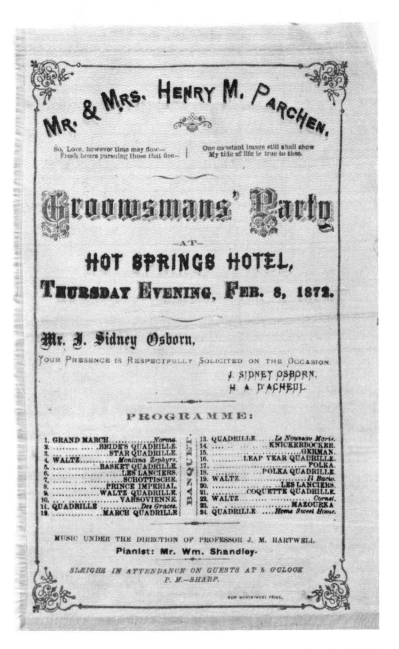

Invitation printed on silk to a groomsman's party given by Miller and H. A. D'Acheul in Montana Territory, 1872.

MARCH 12, 1867

The day opened with the thermometer 27° below zero. At this writing, at half past two it is 16° below zero.

MARCH 17, 1867

Arose at 8 o'clock intending to attend Sunday School. I proceeded to make an elaborate toilet. I was somewhat troubled in regard to one boot, it having a hole in the toe. A needle and some black thread overcame the difficulty however & I came out *bran new* in my best suit. Studied French untill noon, dined at the Planter's House & studied untill two and started out to look for someone to go to Sunday School with. Among all my friends and acquaintances, of whom I met quite a number, I could not find one that would go with me and so great was the ridiculing way in which they spoke of it being good enough for children that I became ashamed of myself for wanting to go and thereupon returned to the store, recited my French lesson to Capt. DeLacy and afterwards supped at the Planter's House. After supper I proceeded to fulfill an engagement made on Wednesday eve at the Amateur Theatrical performance to call upon Miss Fanny Lovell. Arriving at the house I found Mrs. Lovell about to start out for the purpose of assisting in organizing an Episcopal church. I passed a couple of hours very pleasantly, however, with Miss. Fanny, who is a very pretty and interesting girl of fourteen (Feb.), very smart, naive, and intelligent and, withal, a disposition kind and good, at least so thought I. Indeed I am certainly in love with the dear little thing. What *Kind* of love I have been unable to discover but powerful enough to throw me into a fit of the blues and cause another demand upon this my *blue* companion. It seems so hard to have "no one to love now," to caress, to be "roaming along through life's wilderness." 'Tis terrible the blues—for over a year I have escaped them but they have caught me again. I think this is the last attack, however, unless I am stricken by Cupid in some impossible manner.

Of all the young men of my acquaintances I know of none

in so disconsolate a position as myself and yet they all think me lighthearted and convivial & I am always welcomed wherever I go but all is Hollow-Hollow-Hollow. I begin to fear that my proposed trip to Paris will be a lame affair as I have made some losing spec[ulations] lately. I expect my evil monitor is urging me now to leave all my flattering prospects & go off on a sort of wild goose chase but having said that I was going I will not falter if I have to go afoot. The only blessing that I ask is a *"companion du voyage"* for solitude is terrible to one like me subject to the blues.

How I long to hear from home, from my dear sister, my own darling. I wonder if it is possible for a person of my temperament to exist without loving some one. I begin to think that I should try and find somebody to toil with me through life's weary way —and that unless I do I will find some extravagant way of bestowing all the strength of my affections upon some object as poor, puny, and unreliable as the "quicksand" where I have already lost so much that I can never replace. How singularly I am constituted—some persons in my situation would become dissapated, would drink and make noise to drown their thoughts, indeed much better men than I do so for *pleasure.*

I despise such things. It is about as congenial to my senses as would be the idea of taking arsenic in order to go to heaven. There is no sense in over-powering the faculties in order to keep them quiet. A faculty is a curse unless it is made to be *actively beneficial* to ones self. There is nothing negative in a person's brain (if it is at all active) effective either of pleasure or pain. I wonder if God in his wisdom does not give out the problem thus—I placed man upon the earth a simple being. His wants were few and easily satisfied and how little it took to make each day to him one of perfect happiness. He has offended and I will punish him by imparting into him a desire to learn new things which shall give him no happiness.

Thus I often think concerning the "savants" of the world, the know-everythings. Does it bring them happiness? It seems to me that it would be almost an unsatisfactory wedding for me to wed myself to an Art. Living alone for its sake I wonder what place they could have in heaven for such a one. He would not admire the heavenly beauty of the scene because he had left his easel behind & could not produce a copy. And thus I am unhappy. I love art and I want to love somebody and cannot.

The reason is "lucre." I can not devote myself to art. I can not deceive one I love and I must with the Lucre restore myself again *at home.* Prof. Toft[42] also called with me at Mrs. Lovell's. I doubt much however whether he enjoyed his visit as well as I did mine. He is painting me a dozen views of this part of the sphere.

APRIL 6, 1867

Recruited 7 members for the "Union League" this afternoon and missed a French lesson in consequence of attending the meeting in order to see them initiated into the order. I myself became a member about a month since. Engaged Mr. Rockfellow's house. To go to summit tomorrow.

APRIL 7, 1867

At 8½ A.M. proceeded to Mr. R[ockfellow's] stable, saddled Jim, his favorite, and in company with Richmond started for the summit. The road from Va. City to summit winds through Alder Gulch cut along the hill sides and crossing the bottom in several places riding along with the mountains on either side going almost perpendicular to the height of several hundred feet with pine trees dotting the hills here & there in black patches one peak arising above the other. Away in the distance the top of the highest peak was covered with clouds. Below in the gulch the miner's cabins, sluice boxes, shafts, & windlasses, are immense piles of dirt and corresponding holes, all the result of toil for gold, looking as if thrown up in some wallowing "sports" which had taken place. All is deserted and still but speaking with

42 This was the artist Peter Toft (sometimes Tofft or Tufts), a native of Denmark who traveled extensively in the West during the 1860's and 1870's. He was born in 1825 and died in 1901. See Robert Taft, *Artists and Illustrators of the Old West, 1850–1900* (New York, 1953), 307–308.

voices louder than ever could be made by the miners were they there. After reaching summit we tied our horses and proceeded to inspect a tunnel 270 feet long which has been run by Mr. Isaacs in the interest of a New York Company, intending to tap the Kearsage Lode, after which we proceeded to the Mill of Lucas Mining Co., where one half of the mill was running, 6 stamps. This being my first visit to a Quartz Mill I examined it very particularly. After which we proceeded to inspect the shaft of the Lucas Lode.[43] Mr. R[ockfellow] not wishing to go down, I descended alone some 60 feet down a shaft cut in the solid rock, 10 ft. square it had been sunk 110 feet but proving unprofitable to resist the water by man force, they had given at the lower 50 feet to that element and commenced to drift on either side in the direction of the vein of quartz, intending eventually to pump the water by steam power and then sink deeper. After lunching on pickles and bread & tea, the best we could get in the place at 75¢ per head, we mounted again and returned to the mouth of spring gulch and started for Christnott's Mill. The road or gorge along the bottom of which we travelled was covered with snow to the varying depth of two to six feet and of necessity we led our horses over many of the worst places, they sinking to the depth of their body. We finally reached the mill and hunting up Mr. Christnott, he showed us through the works. The machinery which he uses to crush the rocks is what is known as the Chillian Rollers. His works stand as a living testimony to untiring labor and perseverance. Here among the clouds he has erected at an expence of $80,000 a splendid building of stone and filled it with perfectly appointed machinery as well and beautifully put together as in any establishment in the east. Instead of stamps by his method the quartz is put into flat pans about 18 inches deep and four feet broad. Two large rollers weighing from two to three tons which rolled around upon the quartz effectively crush it by a slide in the side of the pan. The Pulverized mass is dropped upon a screen through which it

43 The Lucas Lode was among the richest ore deposits discovered in Montana during 1864.

passes after which it is put into a wrought iron tank about the shape and size of a barrel. Some quicksilver & tin cannon balls are placed therein and by a swift rotary motion the quicksilver and pulp are thoroughly mixed after which the mixture is drawn or allowed to run out into sluice boxes in the bottom of which copper plates catch the quick silver and gold. The balance of the operation consists in gathering the quicksilver & gold & retorting the same.

MAY 9, 1867

Mr. R[ockfellow] greatly surprised me yesterday by asking me if I wanted to go back to Bannack.[44] Of course I did! Traveling on a salary is better than working on the same amount of salary at least for a change. So at 4 o'clock I started this A.M. for Bannack, my business being in chief to Post some bills, to "Go to Salmon River by way of Bannack and Argenta & J. S. Rockfellow Grocery." Riding with the driver I found the weather quite chilly. The road lay over rolling land or "benches" to the valley of the Stinking Water or "Passamaro" River where we stopped at Loraine's to breakfast. Our breakfast was fit for an epicure. Although the bill was not much troubled by diversity of dishes, the beefsteaks were of the tenderest, the eggs of the freshest, the coffee of the purest, and the milk undoubtedly unmixed. Our party consisted of Messrs. Deidesheimer,[45] Brookie, Kirby, Young, Phillips and myself. The road from Loraine's to Massey's Ranch where we breakfasted lay through the Big Hole Valley. After leaving Massey's we crossed through the Beaver head valley, an unproductive mountain valley on the farther side of which—the level at the mouth of the canyon—Black tail deer appeared. Among the features of this level, or plateau, are

[44] Montana's oldest town, located at an elevation of 5,510 feet, was named for the Bannack Indians who once populated the region. Bannack was the first capital of Montana, but by 1865 the capital had been moved to Virginia City.

[45] This was Philip Deidesheimer, the mining engineer. Both the mining technique which he invented and the town of Philipsburg, Montana, were named for him. He moved eventually to Nevada after experiencing a major failure in Montana. Deer Lodge *New Northwest*, November 30, 1877, and December 14, 1877. This Montana paper exulted over his failure in Nevada as well as in Montana.

to the west, Bald Mountain, rising covered with snow to the height of 12,000 feet above the level of the sea, to the south the mountains of the Stinking Water Range.

Before reaching Argenta a storm arose of snow & rain & hail and, unwillingly, I relinquished my seat in front and took the inside of the coach. Argenta is a town of about 3 or 4 hundred inhabitants beautifully laid out upon the level plain at the foot of the Bannack Mountains. Aftear leaving Argenta we commenced to cross the Bannack Range, ascending several of the ascents on foot. We finally reached Bannack and I beheld for the first time the place settled in Montana by the miners of 1863. Supped at Frenchy's on mountain trout, made a hungry man's repast. After supper I spent the balance of the day about equally between Bannack Billiard Saloon and the store.

MAY 10, 1867

Intended to start early to explore the quartz leads at Marysville, a place about a mile from Bannack. Depending upon Mr. Dunlap for guide & companion, I was compelled to wait till after dinner when we proceeded to Marysville.

MAY 26, 1867

At midnight I bade adieu to my kind and liberal employer (for the past two years and one month), Mr. Rockfellow. After writing for me many letters that he thought might be of assistance, he bade me farewell with tears in his eyes and a trembling voice. I hardly thought that my coming or leaving was of so much interest and would affect *anyone* as much—it even brought some drops to my eyes. Well, such is life. I have served him faithfully and have gained from him something more than his money. Tramped through mud and darkness to say goodbye to Mrs. R[ockfellow]. Found her asleep upon the sofa. Posted books untill one o'clock and at two left on the stage for Benton via Helena. Mr. Beattie, Dunbar, Harry, and all the available "force" of the store being present at the departure of the coach, having set up all night for that purpose. Thus commences my "Voyage en Europe." The weather being chilly I took an inside seat. After stopping at Nevada City to take in a woman and baby we rode swiftly toward Helena. It is a magnificently stocked line, this road from Va. City to Helena. It is owned and managed by those princes of stagers, Wells Fargo & Co. Every horse employed is a perfect sample of horse flesh, of large size, American breed, fat, well kept, and the teams well matched. Arrived at Helena at 8 o'clock, having rode 124 miles in 18 hours. Walked up a hill or two and breakfasted at 4 A.M. and dined at 1 P.M., fasting 8 hours, the only item of unpleasantness.

HELENA, MAY 27, 1867

Geo. W. Ware having *insisted* upon it, I am making his store, Ware, Ellis & Co., my headquarters and sleeping apartment while in this city. Having duly breakfasted with the aforesaid Geo. at his mess, I started out on a voyage of discovery. Called at the several banks to let them know that I was ready to carry treasure through to Omaha. Only succeeded in getting $3500 from Hershfield & Co. for which I received the sum of $75. Having received $35 for another shipment from Hanaeur at Va. City, I have secured part of my expense, at least, to the states.[46] Mr. Jno. Ming, who pressed me into his service for dinner, met "ye local" of the Post who informed me that Ben Dittes[47] was not around.

[46] L. H. Hershfield & Co. were the leading bankers in Montana before the rise of William Andrews Clark. A. Hanauer was Hershfield's Virginia City partner. Hanauer to Hershfield, May 21, 1867: "Mr. Osborn, bookkeeper for Rockfellow, will start for the states by river which will be a good chance to send Dust, if you have any. . . . Osborn will call on you." May 23, 1865: "If you send any dust with Osborn you will have to allow him something; he thinks about 2%." (Hershfield & Co. Papers, May, 1867, Correspondence, Montana Historical Society). On May 28, 1867, Hershfield replied to Hanauer: "I sent down with Mr. Osborn 225 ounces dust [which] don't leave Fort Benton before the 5th. If I had known that, would have sent same by Express in preference." (Hershfield & Co. Papers, Virginia City Box, 1867, Montana Historical Society). This correspondence refers to the gold Miller took east.

[47] By 1867, Helena boasted a population of approximately five thousand persons, and many of Miller's merchant friends had already begun to move their businesses there or to Deer Lodge. Among these was John H. Ming, who had a new store at No. 8 Main Street, Helena. He advertised in the Helena *Rocky Mountain Gazette.* Dittes, co-owner of Virginia City's *Montana Post,* commenced another journal in Helena, *The Tri-Weekly Republican.*

He, however, together with Cole Saunders,[48] the Col's brother, made me very comfortable and rendered me much valuable assistance in getting specimens of minerals. Helena I found to be the finest city in Montana. It has, I should judge, about 5,000 inhabitants (quite considerable portion of which are jews) & is well built, as is usually the case, in a ravine or gulch. The stores along the chief business street are usually built very respectably in style and size, quite a number of them being of stone, two or three stories high, with plate glass doors, windows, etc. About the street entrances, to the second and third stories upon the walls, the slips of tin present an appearance very like unto "Gotham."[49] At 12 o'clock my friend Ware and myself could have been found at an oyster saloon diligently paying our respects to "Field's Steamed."[50] At 12 o'clock I was in the arms of Murphy [Morpheus].

MAY 28, 1867

At 2 ½ o'clock I was awakened by "Knocking at my chamber door." Proceeding to the stage office of Huntly's Line and waiting "dilligently" for half an hour we were duly arranged, myself and five others—I upon seat with the driver, bidding adieu to Ware. The crack of the driver's whip started four splendid American horses and away we sped. I had the enjoyment of a *good* cigar on a trip of 20 hours, as the advertisement says. My credentials, consisting of a bottle of whiskey and bunch of cigars, being duly presented to the driver, he enlivened the *very early* hours of the morning by describing to me his various exploits in the "Jehu" line of business. A very pleasant man he

48 Cole Saunders also became prominent in Helena as a wholesale trader and was later superintendent of the Marie Mine at Philipsburg. See Leeson, *History of Montana*, 704, 737, and Deer Lodge *New Northwest*, December 5, 1891.

49 Miller meant that the metal store fronts made the architecture resemble that in New York.

50 This expensive brand of canned oysters sold for $24.00 a dozen in 1864. By 1867, the price at Virginia City had fallen to $16.00. During this period prices on other foodstuffs were also dropping steadily. Flour which sold as high as $1.00 per pound in 1864 fell to $80 per hundred pounds. See Ronan, "Memoirs," 65. On bread riots in Virginia City see the Diary of Isaac Rogers, April 18, 1865. Missouri Historical Society, St. Louis.

seemed to us at starting. But, alas for appearances, our smiles were turned to frowns, our good humor to wrath, our good opinion to positive dislike—long before we reached Fort Benton. With most diabolical persistency he continually sang out upon reaching any mud hole: "Now gentlemen if you will be so kind as to give me a lift for only 20 steps," this meaning that we were to walk through the mud and water from one to two miles, and in one case, four. The first station bore the euphoneus name Silver Heels, a station consisting of fifteen houses and four tents. Here we change horses, taking, in place of our splendid American stock, a six-horse team of wild "cayuses." Our driver, in throwing upon the seat some stones, accidently struck our whiskey bottle and, "alas poor Yorik," our troubles had commenced. From this station on I found myself an important iota of the working forces of the establishment, my attention being constantly directed to the two leader horses whom I continually pelted with the stones to no little damage to their hides. Leaving the station half an hour behind time, our road crossed a plateau almost level at the end of which, ten or fifteen miles distant, we entered a Kanyon at the entrance to which we crossed a very steep hill. Here of course the passengers had to walk. In doing so one of them shot a grouse. The effect of the explosion was very fine, the sound being repeated several times and finally dying away in the far distance. Before reaching the station we made 5 miles in 26 minutes. Here we breakfasted, the breakfast being very good, as good as an average one in the states. From this station we drove rapidly, soon reaching the Kanyon through which the toll road of King & Gillette[51] is cut and soon we were threading its length. It is quite a considerable piece of work, completed with great labor and cost. Its entire length was made by excavations, embankments, wedging, and grading. It is a grand gorge eight miles long. The rocks on either side often rise to a height to a thousand feet, almost perpendicularly, sometimes

[51] King & Gillette were originally freighters of goods from Fort Benton to Helena. See Stout, *Montana Story*, I, 288, and advertisements of their Helena store in the *Montana Post*.

almost meeting above the road. The face of the clifts is oftimes broken by the forge of the water which has some seams deep into it, thus separating the rock, leaving portions standing out in bold relief, looking very much like turrets, battlements, towers, and steeples. With the rushing torrent beneath us our road cut into and along the side of the mountain, with the wild horses sometimes dragging the coach dangerously near the edge, a fall down which would have been decidedly unpleasant. It was a scene to be remembered. In crossing a slough near the end of the Kanyon, our vehicle "stuck fast." "All out," was the cry, including myself. In crossing a narrow neck of ground between two ponds of water (in order to belay a stubborn mule), the ground gave way and I was in an instant engulphed into the water, saving my hat in dryness *alone* of all my garments. I crawled forth amid a hearty peal of laughter from the passengers (in which I heartily joined) at my ludicrous appearance. I stripped and wound about me a blanket which was fortunately dry and, hanging my clothes upon the top of the stage, I mused upon "the uncertainty of Life." I was exempt from any further walking however untill we arrived at the next driving station—Kennedy's—where I donned my clothes. Still wet I ate heartily of a good meal. After leaving this station we drove through a river which, owing to the spring floods, was in a very turbulent state. When in the centre our coach entered a hole. The horses refused to pull and came very near upsetting the coach. In the course of their plunging we were obliged to climb from the coach upon the backs of some horses which the ranchman brought to our aid and in this manner safely effected a crossing. The coach, relieved of our weight, was pulled across and on we started—only four or five hours late. Our route now lay over hills and benches, going in all directions and making wide detours in order to circumvent some unpassable hill. Hour after hour passed on. The station did not appear. The horses *would walk* and as it gradually grew darker the driver became more dangerous. After coming very near upsetting us the driver lost his self-possession and began to say that he had passed the station in the dark. Our lucky star was still in the ascendant however. At half past ten we crossed the line of Bird's Tail Rock (named because it did *not* resemble a bird's tail) and shortly after reached the station. Here we had naturally supposed our troubles would be ended. Quite different however was the case. A station without a roof or floor, except enough to protect the stove and table of the station keeper, the rain coming down, with that steady quiet manner which makes the wet felt before it touches you. It was *almost* as bad as driving in the coach. However we secured a tolerable supper and, after digging ditches around our beds to prevent the rain from attacking us on all sides at once, I turned in with Major Davis of Stuart's Cavalry, C. S. A. Spreading my overcoat and blankets upon the ground, and using his blankets and shawl for a covering, with my traveling bag for a pillow (containing $7,000 in gold dust), I slept sweetly after the exhausting efforts of the day. I found our party was one eminently a type of those traveling in the far west since the close of the war. It consisted of six persons. Major Geo. Clinton was our leader in esprit and the party was constantly convulsed with peals of laughter at his fortunate hits. His spirits never flagged during the whole of the trip and his presence was a valuable aid to the rest of us in killing the time. He held the high and honorable position of Indian Agent at Fort Benton. He was ably seconded in his efforts by Major A. M. S. Carpenter, an old acquaintance of mine in Virginia City who, having been appointed collector of the revenue at Benton, and also a major in the volunteers to transport ammunition from Camp Cook to the Gallatin, was en-route to take possession of his office. His commission was from General Meagher.[52] Major Davis, my very agreeable companion of the night, fought during the rebellion in the cavalry command of Genl. Stuart. By his side was a gentleman who fought equally zealously in the union ranks. A professional gambler of the cut-throat order completed the party.

[52] In 1867, Carpenter was also appointed superintendent of schools by General Meagher. See Stout, *Montana Story*, I, 493–94.

MAY 29, 1867

At 5 o'clock we were drummed out of our comfortable beds in the mud by the ranchman in order to take coach. We accordingly took our places but alas for anticipations and hopes we were doomed to remain there all day. The stock, being lost during the night, did not arrive untill noon, and then in very bad and exhausted condition and unable to proceed untill the next morning. The question now arose: How shall we pass the day? We shot at marks with our revolvers (each of us had one) listened to the ravings of Carpenter and Wright, called heaven's choicest blessings upon the weather, the stage line, and the world generally. For our especial comfort and convenience it again commenced to rain, and the wet being added to other miseries, I in disgust spread my blankets and slept through the latter part of the day. At night I took the ground and mud under the table for my bed & slept.

MAY 30, 1867

Got off at 10 o'clock. Rolled as far as Sun River[53] where we arrived at about one o'clock. Here, leaving our heavy coach, the cause of half our miseries, we secured a light wagon and rolled happily forward. Reached Benton at about 1 o'clock in the morning. A tolerable supper proved very acceptable after which the Union soldier and myself secured a bed together and slept.

MAY 31, 1867

Slept late. Up at 11 o'clock. My first proceeding was to deposit my cash at Melton & Taylor's for safe keeping. Found numerous friends & made many acquaintances.

JUNE 1, 1867

Passed the day very agreeably, the greater portion of it being spent in reading in the library belonging to Carroll & Steell[54]

53 The Sun River flows into the Missouri near Great Falls, Montana.
54 Mathew Carroll and George Steell, onetime clerks of the American Fur Company, built their own store of sawed logs in 1864, and the firm became one

a very good one for the mountains, containing many works of merit & interest. Among the rest I was particularly interested in "Pencillings By The Way" by Geo. P. Willis and "Travelings in Central America" by Genl. Thomas F. Meagher. Geo. Ware having arrived by coach, he requested me to show my cabinet of mineral specimens to Major Hubbard of the W. W. Five Co. Accordingly, I proceeded to the Fort and was introduced to some half a dozen of the Major's friends and appointed 10 o'clock tomorrow to receive them. The town of Fort Benton I have found to consist of a collection of adobe houses, and large wooden storehouses (used in the spring for storing the great quantities of goods arriving from the east by river). The former are in sufficient numbers to contain a resident population of about 150 inhabitants.[55] The fort proper, which is situated a short distance from a village, is considered to be the best built of any upon the upper Missouri river. Strong adobe walls about ten feet high and three feet thick enclose a space of about three acres of open court around the sides of which are erected the trading store and quarters for officers and attaches of the company. The four sides are commanded by two towers permitting a full sweep to a number of small field pieces.

The "Miner" arrived at about sundown from St. Louis, it being thus the second boat up this year, the "Waverly" having arrived six days since and returned to Camp Cook, about 200 miles down the river, in order to bring up troops for this post. On the "Miner's" arrival about half a dozen field pieces were dragged to the edge of the river and a salute was fired. The river,

of the most successful at Fort Benton. On this trade see Paul F. Sharp, *Whoop-Up Country, The Canadian-American West, 1865–1885* (Minneapolis, 1955), 213–14; also Stout, *Montana Story,* I, 215. The firm advertised regularly in the *Montana Post,* and their possession of a significant library at so remote a place as Fort Benton is notable.

[55] Fort Benton, "The Chicago of the Plains," was located at the head of steam navigation only a few miles from the great falls of the Missouri River, or "Great Muddy." It was established in 1846 and named after Thomas Hart Benton. Probably the most cosmopolitan town on the plains, this inland post became the commercial hub of the Upper Missouri country. The so-called Whoop-Up Trail to Fort McLeod, 240 miles northward in Canada, began at Fort Benton. Traffic down the Missouri to the Mississippi also began there.

running along a narrow valley or basin, with high bluffs on either side, the effect was beautifull, the explosions being followed by echo after echo and finally dying away in the far distance.

IV

FORT BENTON TO NEW YORK

JUNE 2, 1867

The weather is very warm, the sun almost scorching a person. At the appointed hour showed my cabinet to a dozen or more of admiring guests. Among them was D. K. Allen, correspondant of the Chicago *Republican* who was much delighted with them. Accepted an invitation and dined on board the "Miner" with Capt. Hubble. The "Waverly" arriving from Camp Cook, I engaged a cabin passage for $100. After supper proceeded to the boat and slept.

JUNE 3, 1867

Weather still beautifull. The steamer started at half past 10 o'clock, the "Miner" starting out ahead. Among the passengers were 2 half breed Indian boys who are to be educated in the states. They made frantic efforts to reach the shore and cried as if their hearts would break at leaving their wild mountain country. As we left Fort Benton we fired a farewell shot and shortly after, behind the first bend of the river, the fort disappeared from our sight. River very high and we sped rapidly along. Passed several boats during the day creeping slowly up the river. Some of them seemed scarcely to move, so strong was the current in places. River very crooked and scenery monotonous. By turns bottom lands covered with cottonwoods & small ledges of crumbling limestone and clay hills. Very dreary and uninviting indeed. At 5 o'clock we reached Camp Cook where are stationed about 200 soldiers in a locality where they are perfectly useless for all military purposes, owing to the nature of the ground behind the fort and also between the fort and the river. In the spring during the wet season they can not move at all and during the dry season only in one direction—toward the river. We here saw some fine horses, the property of the U. S. but in the possession of the officers. The barracks are built upon the level plateau which here extends on either side of the river in the form of a square. Very substantially and securely constructed for the safety and comfort of the troops. Among the attractions of the place is a theatre where amateur dramaticals are offered by the officers and men occasionally. We here passed the "Miner," she having been stopped by the government officials. After remaining about 2 hours at Camp Cook we dropped down the river about 10 miles or more where we tied up, the hands taking in wood. Passed the "Cora." The hills back of Fort Cook are called Cooleys.

JUNE 4, 1867

This morning a negro, one of the boat hands, fell overboard. No effort was made to save him and he sank to rise no more, the crew standing about watching for him to rise. Having discovered the excellence of the view, from the same I spent most of the day in the wheel house. Passed a herd of buffalo & saw hundreds of wild geese with their young. They did not attempt to fly away as our boat approached, but sinking their bodies into

Miller *c.* 1880, after he had moved to Dakota Territory.

J. K. P. Miller Building, one of the first brick buildings constructed in Deadwood, Dakota Territory, in the 1880's. Building was located next to the Deadwood National Bank.

Courtesy Miller family

the water floated in foolish security, leaving only their heads visible. Passed Fort Hawley,[1] a post erected last year for the purpose of trading with the Indians. Passed the point and saw the remains of a trading post erected by Steel and burned by the Indians. Passed the "Yorktown" and "Mountaineer" on the last of which I saw Billy Childs and his newly elected wife. The boats, both upward and downward bound, are this year filled with families, some going home to educate their children or flying to the comforts not to be found in the Rockey Mountains. Others are coming up river to meet their husbands who have gone ahead and prepared homes for them. One Jew and his wife came up on the "Waverly" and, after looking about Fort Benton for a week, concluded that Montana was not the place for him. Accordingly he hired himself to the same boat and is at present engaged in packing wood from the flats or peeling potatoes, as the case may be.

JUNE 6, 1867

Started at 2 o'clock. We have the most indefatigable of captains, P. H. Rea. Passed Round Butte about 2 hours after starting. It is in shape very much like a Canadian's hat of the peaked variety and of about as imposing appearance. At about 10 o'clock the sudden reversion of the engines and sharp whistling proclaiming "Something Up," I dropped an abstract of mining property which I was engaged in copying in the dining room and, rushing on deck, found the entire force of the boat engaged (such as had guns) in shooting buffalo. Four youthfull members of that Liperthus [?] race, attempting to cross the river, found themselves directly in front of the steamer. They were terribly frightened and endeavored to reach the shore, which they did. But the banks were so steep that they were unable to ascend them. They were accordingly butchered without any difficulty al-

[1] Fort Hawley was built by Louis Rivet of the Northwest Fur Company in 1866 and named after A. F. Hawley, a partner in that company. It was established for trade with the Gros Ventres Indians and was located a few miles below Fort Benton on the south side of the Missouri River and some twenty miles above Musselshell.

though many shots were fired before the desired result was obtained. It made me pity them to see their frantic efforts to escape and the storm of bullets with which they were saluted. After they were killed, or badly wounded, the steamer's yawl was lowered and, rowing to the sides of the enormous carcasses, towed them to the side of the steamer where they were hoisted aboard and duly skinned & cleaned for the table. After dinner in rounding a sandbar a couple herds of Antelope were discovered. Before they could get away one of them had his leg broken by a bullet. Unable to run, he quietly awaited the approach of the yawl and submitted to having his throat cut. Thus by our success today it is ensured that our larder will not be slim before we reach Saint Louis, as far as fresh meat is concerned. Our table on the steamer is thus far most excellent. Tender beef, light bread, and good coffee. Our steamer is also well supplied with the softer sex. Among the misseses are Miss Mathers, Alexandre & Hutchison. The scenery today is improving greatly. We are now passing beautifull bottom lands, sometimes thickly covered with cottonwood lumber. A striking peculiarity of these trees is the seeming rows in which they stand. Anon we pass immense flat bottoms covered with willows stretching off in the distance to ranges of bluffs gradually rising untill they form the horizon line, the lowest being hardly above the flats. Shortly after dinner we passed a war party of Indians about 75 in number. An Indian on board signified that they were war Indians by going through the pantomine of killing a man, cutting his throat, and scalping him. Fortunately the deep water was on the opposite side to that on which they stood and we did not become better acquainted. Passed a large herd of buffalo and numbers of antelope too far distant to shoot at. Weather delightfully pleasant, the sun being clouded just sufficiently to prevent too much heat. The river begins to widen in places and is hardly as crooked as heretofore. Passed Cook's Point where stands a cabin or two and is kept a wood yard. A short distance below here the greatest bend in the river occurs, the river going round a neck of land, making a detour of over fifteen miles and returning to within one hundred yards of the starting place. Met the "Ida Stockdale" laid up with a crack in her boiler. Spent an hour after supper in the pilot house with Miss Mathers and Smith, her gardien for the voyage. Taking my "Autocrat of the Breakfast Table" I endeavoured to read in the cabin, was interrupted first by Miss Mathers & secondly by Dr. Glick who was taken with a fit of cramps. Assisted in applying about half a pound of chloreform to him. At 11 o'clock I prevailed upon the steward to give me some pine apple, cheese, & crackers for lunch after which I slept, the boat in the mean time having tied up to a piece of timber land where a passenger shot at a beaver but missed him.

JUNE 7, 1867

As usual started at daylight. The scenery still changing, flat lands & bluffs being now about evenly divided. Passed a party of Indians drawn up near a wood pile in line awaiting our approach in order to "Swap." Weather still delightfull, a cool breeze and warm sun—the component parts of fine weather. The "Miner" reached us at half past 10 o'clock A.M. While we were wooding the hands were immediately called in and a sharp trial of speed took place which was soon brought to a close by the collision of our boat with the bank of the river, thereby disabling one of the paddle wheels and causing a detention of four hours before the boat could be rendered fit to proceed. We then steamed to Fort Union, which point was reached about half past 7 P.M., 787 miles from Ft. Benton and 2327 miles from St. Louis.[2] Fort Union is a trading post established in 1857 by Pierre Chouteau of whom a portrait is still to be seen painted upon the outside facade of the central building inside of the fort, which is of the usual square shape & with the customary adobe walls and

[2] Fort Union was 1,782 miles from St. Louis according to the U. S. Engineers' survey of 1890 cited in Bernard De Voto, *Across the Wide Missouri* (Cambridge, Mass., 1957), 429. The river, however, has constantly shortened its course. Located at the junction of the Missouri and Yellowstone rivers, Union was one of the finest military posts in the American West. It was a gathering place for furs from the major river basins east of the Rocky Mountains. Hiram M. Chittenden, *The American Fur Trade* (3 vols., New York, 1902), III, 958–60; Frank B. Harper, *Fort Union and Its Neighbors on the Upper Missouri* (St. Paul, 1925).

towers commanding the approaches. The Indians, of whom there were a great many lounging about the fort, were well worth looking at in their picturesque costumes. During the afternoon a wind & rain storm made the Hurricaine deck untenable. Spent the evening in the cabin chatting with Miss M[athers].

JUNE 7, 1867 [Miller wrote two entries under this date.]

Started at sunrise. Arose too late for a first or second table and found the third table miserable. Also found the wash room miserable. Making known my troubles to the steward he forth with gave Mr. Morrison and myself a towell and soap to ourselves and permission to wash with the officers. Heavy wind storm all day. Cold, chilly, and uncomfortable. My favourite position has been behind and near the smoke stack where it was warm and protected from the wind. We are now only 20 or 30 miles from the British possessions.[3] Was installed as head of the table today, Mrs. Tutt on my left and Miss Mathers upon my right. Passed White Earth River at 1½ P.M. Passed 3 boats, among them the "Abyona" at 6 o'clock 30 miles above Fort Berthold,[4] shortly after which we grounded on a series of sand bars and laid up for the night in company with 2 other boats.

JUNE 8, 1867

Started at daylight. Our first exploit was to run into the "G. A. Thompson," smashing their cook house into small pieces and seriously disarranging their breakfast, which was being cooked, distributing potatoes, beef, and bread upon the river rather freely. Passed Knife River[5] at 10 minutes past 12, a *river* about 10 feet wide at the mouth. Reached Fort Berthold at 10 A.M. at which place we again passed the irrepressible "Miner."

3 The Missouri River runs from west to east at this point.

4 Fort Berthold, constructed in 1845 by the American Fur Company, was named after Bartholomew Berthold, a Tyrolese emigré who first came to America in 1798. He became a partner of Auguste Chouteau and a prominent merchant and fur trader at St. Louis. Annie Heloise Abel, *Chardon's Journal at Fort Clark, 1834–39* (Pierre, 1932), 250 n.

5 Knife River is in present-day North Dakota.

At this fort are stationed about 100 troops. About 1000 Indians were near the place. We were refused admittance into the square or blockhouse. Passed the "Little Rock" at 5 o'clock P.M.

JUNE 9, 1867

Reached Fort Rice at about 10 o'clock.[6] At Fort Rice are stationed about 700 Regulars. It is situated upon a level plateau on the south bank of the river. There is also here a first class trading post, the first we have seen as yet. A number of Indian burial places were distributed about the place. They were quite interesting to me. A platform resting upon four poles about 15 feet from the ground supported a box painted red or the body of the person in upright position only protected from the weather by skins and clothes. Purchased here a box of cigars & 2 lbs. of figs, believing that I had been unhappy long enough. The country continually improves in character, the bluffs having entirely ceased. In their place rolling land is covered with beautifull verdure of deep rich green. The trees too are changing, the ash appearing in considerable numbers although only of the large sapling order. Stopped at 6 o'clock to "wood up." On the boat are about 50 discharged soldiers. Adding their forces to those of the crew a large quantity of wood was soon on board. Here we camped for the night. Mr. Morrison favoured me today with a short account of his exploits in Montana, resulting in a net profit to him of about $15,000 after working 2 years. His brother is at present traveling in France. He showed me his photograph and requested me to make myself known to him in case we should meet. Passed the bank today where the Indians attacked the "Big Horn" and killed one man, while wooding a few weeks since.

6 Fort Rice was erected in 1864 on the right bank of the Missouri six and one-half miles above the mouth of the Cannonball. This military reservation was carved out of the lands of the Uncpapa Sioux in 1864, within present-day North Dakota, by six companies of the Thirtieth Wisconsin Volunteers. *Forty Years a Fur Trader on the Upper Missouri, the Personal Narrative of Charles Larpenteur, 1833–1872*, ed. by Elliot Coues (2 vols., New York, 1899), II, 384 n.; Hiram Martin Chittenden, *History of Early Steamboat Navigation on the Missouri River* (2 vols., New York, 1903), II, 260.

JUNE 10, 1867

Weather warm. Wind high. It blew so fiercely that the boat was turned round and round, frequently driving us against the bank. We were finally forced to tie up. While there the "Only Chance" passed us. We have passed considerable fine grazing country. On each side of the river a flat bottom land, varying in width from one to three miles, is succeeded by small elevations of land covered with mountain grass and rather more gravelly soil is seen. We have on board a man and his wife, both crazy and labouring under the delusion that each night they are to be killed. A soldier, taken with delirium tremens, is howling hideously below the hurricaine deck upon which I am watching the sun set. Four of the ladies, Misses Alexander, Hutchison, Mathews, and Mrs. Tutt have just gone below. Sunset not particularly fine. Indeed I have not seen one since our departure.

JUNE 11, 1867

Ran untill one o'clock this morning, the effects of which were plainly visible this morning in the "situation." We had passed the "Only Chance" and were running abreast of the "Miner," which we shortly passed also. Passed Fort Sully during the night.[7] Met quite a number of Indians in small parties during the morning. Passed Crow Agency at 9 o'clock. Had a long conversation with Mr. McAllister of St. Louis who has just returned from Europe. Passed the Bijoux Hills, a collection of small conical elevations of ground. Passed Fort Randall, which is situated some distance from the river on the south bank.[8] Still further improvement in the country. Shortly after sundown reached Choteau Agency where, for the first time since leaving Benton, I saw some signs of cultivation. Saw the sunset from

7 The original Fort Sully was built in 1863 by order of General Alfred Sully about four and one-half miles below Pierre, South Dakota. A new Fort Sully was constructed in 1866 thirty miles higher up the river and was situated within a 27,000-acre reservation. Larpenteur, *Forty Years a Fur Trader*, II, 357 n.

8 General William S. Harney established Fort Randall, an Indian rendezvous and military post, in 1855. See Writers' Program, South Dakota, *South Dakota Place Names* (Vermillion, 1941), 641.

the Hurricaine deck again. A moonlight night. Soldiers singing upon open deck while the vessel glides smoothly and swiftly along. "Ever of Thee," first time I have heard it since in 1860 by Louisa Simons. It was a beautiful night, a beautiful moon and millions of twinkling stars made each eddy which the boat floated over plainly visible. The soldiers sang very well and we had a delightfull evening.

JUNE 12, 1867

Shortly after sunrise passed Yankton.[9] Breakfast not very palatable. Neither butter nor milk being provided. This morning the song of the bird is heard for the first time in a long time from the dense forest upon either bank. Country growing more settled. Yankton boasts 1200 inhabitants. Have thus far passed 47 boats. Beautifull groves of cottonwood trees among which the birds are singing merrily & beautifull farms upon the flats. Passed Sioux City and reached Decatur. Tied up to the opposite bank intending to remain from 6 in the afternoon untill 7 next day to clean out the boilers of the engines. After supper the steward and about half a dozzen of the passengers, volunteers, among whom was I, took the yawl and crossed the river to Decatur in search of butter, eggs, etc. I took the occasion to invest considerable in candy at a penny a stick; it seemed so marvelously cheap. Returned to the boat well-laden with the articles, having purchased the butter at .25¢. Quite different from the price at Benton, where we paid $2.50 per lb.

JUNE 13, 1867

Intolerably hot during the night untill 1 o'clock when a cool breeze sprang up. Untill then the state rooms were insufferable close. Had another talk with McAllister about Europe. He is very illiterate, pronounces "de" "dee" and visited neither Venice, Strasburgh, Dresden nor Vienna. Crazy man worse this morn-

---

[9] Yankton, South Dakota, was speedily populated by whites after 1858, when a treaty with the Yankton Sioux Indians resulted in the relinquishment of their lands in this area.

ing. We thought of taking his arms away from him, he having a gun and revolver. Passed 2 sunken steamers. Nothing but pilot house visible. Very high wind turned the boat around, sometimes half a dozzen times in rapid succession. Passed Florence, 15 miles above Omaha, and arrived at Omaha about 8 o'clock in the evening, we having come from Benton in 10 days and 10 hours. It was quite dark. I seized my carpet bag and, taking $550 in dust which I have been carrying for Hershfield & Co., carried it to the city, a wearisome task as the express office by which I wished to ship was fully a mile from the steamboat landing. Afterwards I proceeded to the telegraph office and was walking quietly along towards the steamboat when, unluckily, I met Ferris the clerk, Morrison, and one of the pilots of the "Waverly," Chas. A. Wiseman. A drink followed at Shoaf's Billiard Saloon, a beautifull hall with 12 tables and a splendid bar. Wiseman challenged me to a game of billiards, after which we proceeded towards the steamboat landing and found that we were left behind. Making the most of the situation, we have determined to try and catch the "Waverly." Took passage on the "Stonewall" & slept tolerable. Charley could not sleep at all. He was so mortified at being left while he was an officer of the boat.

JUNE 14, 1867

Up at 5½ o'clock. Passed Oreapolis situated on a high steep bank upon the south side of the river among the trees that are thickly set in the bank and are at this time heavily laden with folliage. Passed Plattsmouth and Liberty, the latter once intended to rival Omaha but now containing only three houses of one story each. Reached Nebraska City 9:15 A.M. Found that the "Waverly" had passed here at 5 A.M. Nebraska City, like Omaha, is situated some distance from the river owing to the marshy nature of the flat along the riverbank. Each also is roomy with fine broad streets and many respectably sized buildings although none are remarkable for architectural beauty of design or finish. Lost half an hour at Nebraska City. The "Stonewall" upon which we are travelling is a fine boat with perfect appointments, a good table, and for a clerk the most respectable of snobs. Wiseman gave me a short history of the Missouri River Pilot Association, of which he is a member. 5% of the salary of each member is paid and each one supported when he grows old & poor out of funds thus accumulated. Stalls were erected along the banks of the river in which to deposit notes of changes in the river bed & sand bars. Charley, after calling at 50 stalls, had only found a tack in any of them. Magnificent hilly slopes alternately upon either bank of the river covered with a brilliant green foliage looking refreshingly new after the bleak scenery of Montana. We pass every eight or ten miles beautifull little settlements built among the foliage upon the steep slope of the river, with each house built upon a knoll of its own only partly visible among the trees and looking charmingly new and unsullied. Each soldier aboard the boat carried a paper called a final statement with which he expected to secure his wages in St. Louis. It became quite customary on board to call a soldier "final statement."

JUNE 15, 1867

Reached St. Joseph at about 6 A.M. Leaving the "Stonewall"[10] here we proceeded to the Pacific Hotel and breakfasted. Here at this same hotel 3 years ago was I with about the same amount of cash, $2,000, then bound west—now for the east but not now with the *same* $2,000, the first having been lost long ago in the City of the Saints. Had a good breakfast, the first since leaving the mountains. St. Joseph seems to have grown amazingly since 1864. I find it a city at present worthy of considerable attention and *then* it looked small. Many complaints are made of dull trade. At 11 o'clock we started for Leavenworth, taking the Northern Missouri R. R. from St. Joseph to Weston, thence by ferry at $1.00 apiece fare to Leavenworth. Beautifull country

10 A few years later the steamer *Stonewall*, on which Miller took passage, was involved in a terrible disaster in which two hundred lives were lost. This led to the passage of the Steamboat Act of 1871 regulating safety conditions on board such vessels. Louis C. Hunter, *Steamboats on the Western Rivers* (Cambridge, Mass., 1949), 440.

through here. Grasshoppers thick. Reached Leavenworth at 2½ o'clock.[11] Dined at the Planter's House. Found the dining room downstairs. Pretty waiter girls and excellent victuals although too late for the best dinner. A very respectable looking house. After dinner I tried to sell 2 oz. of gold dust and found every one "on the swindle." Met my friend, who offered to go to Jerusalem with me, and let me have 2 oz. at $21, a loss of about $4 per oz., the result of my being left at Omaha. Left Leavenworth at 4 o'clock. Had to run a long distance to catch the train, owing to the delay in selling the gold dust. Two drunken men were the main feature of the car in which we were forced to ride. Some of their expressions were quite ludicrous, one especially—"To the devil with poverty. Bring on another drink." We had taken 2 seats facing each other so that we could each look out of the window, leaving a vacant place by the side of us. Suddenly, without warning, the two drunkards, leaving their seats, took the two vacant seats by our sides and one of them, rubbing his feet against Charley, soiled his clothes. This was one drop too much and immediately after the offense he seized them each and threw them half the length of the car in either direction and then quietly took his seat amid the plaudits of the passengers. Reaching Jefferson City, we found that the "Waverly" had passed 10 hours ago. Hence we gave up all idea of catching the steamer and took passage for St. Louis.

JUNE 16, 1867

Misfortunes never come singly. A bridge out of order made us tramp about a mile and delayed us a couple of hours. This is a beautifull country through which we are passing. Everything looks so fresh, green, and alive in the vegetable kingdom. The chimneys to many of the houses are built outside of the house. Passed and crossed the Gasconade Bridge where on the opening

11 Leavenworth had in recent years become a new center for outfitters and merchants formerly located at Independence, Westport, Weston, and St. Joseph, Missouri. Many of these moved to Leavenworth, whose proximity to the fort of the same name gave it military protection and made it the commercial terminus for roads radiating from the West.

of the R. R. a horrible accident happened about 6 years ago by which 57 St. Louis citizens were killed.

ST. LOUIS, JUNE 17, 1867

Reached St. Louis about 2 hours ahead of the "Waverly" yesterday. Stepped aboard at the dock. Found that Morrison had taken good care of my effects, including about $1500 in gold dust which I had left in my room.[12] We went to the Southern Hotel and took rooms. Was shown around by Charley. Looked at the ruins of the Lindel House. Today I took a bath, bought some clean linen, and delivered some of my letters. Met Mr. Bush and proceeded to the Mercantile Library, thence to the Dorris Row and about the city generally. Called upon the Field Brothers and delivered J[ohn] S. R[ockfellow]'s letter to them. They were very pleased to see someone from their old employer. Met Joe Doudal, now married, and returning to the hotel I borrowed a pair of opera glasses and went to see the "Black Crook."[13] I found that the play was one which owed its popularity to the scenic effects, the beautifull dancing, and the scant amount of clothing covering the dancer. Among the most beautifull scenes was one in which a literal river of water appeared colored red & looking very like a river of blood which it was intended to represent. Visited the Court House.

JUNE 18, 1867

I found after my return from the "Black Crook" last night that I will be short of money and perhaps will be unable to leave in the morning for New York. I also found that the jewelry store where I borrowed the opera glasses will not open in time to refund my $10 which I left as security for their safe return. The

[12] It will be recalled that Miller had deposited some of his $7,000 in gold with the telegraph office at Omaha. He had carried with him another unspecified amount and had left about $1,500 in gold aboard the *Waverly*.

[13] The American actor, Charles M. Barras, was the author of this very popular drama about sorcery and witchcraft. *The Black Crook: A Most Wonderful History. Now being Performed With Immense Success in All the Principal Theatres Throughout the United States* (Philadelphia, 1866). The play greatly impressed Miller, who refers to it later in the diary.

clerk of the hotel, however, has agreed to take the glasses for $10 in payment of my board. Thus I was enabled to purchase a through ticket and have $2 left. Anxiety, however, destroyed my sleep. With $1800 worth of gold dust in my possession I will probably be unable to purchase a meal! Left the Southern Hotel at 6 o'clock A.M. Purchased a ticket by the Baltimore and Ohio Rail Road for $36 to New York & Washington. The Southern Hotel is one of the finest I have ever seen. As regards its dining room it is without an equal in the United States, 90 x 50 ft. and with a ceiling 27 feet high with 2 mirrors, 5 beautifull chandeliers, and the ceiling is beautifull heavy pannel work. It strikes one upon entering at once with surprise at its beauty and size. The R. R. having provided an omnibus, we started across the river and took the cars. For 60 miles our route lay through a fine farming country after which we came to considerable tracts of wild, uncultivated land. They tell me that the immense German immigration is rapidly filling up the country about here and that land has doubled in price within the 2 weeks past. An old farmer told me that very little trouble was experienced here in managing the darkeys since they have become free. Crazy man brought in. At Vincennes crossed the line into Indiana from Illinois. The cry among the peanutstands was "Boiled Eggs" and "Gooseberry Pie." Among the passengers was a pill doctor who forthwith attached himself to an honest farmer who, however had too much sense, or too little money, to purchase his remedies. About Metchel the scenery much improved along river. Passed 2 tunnels, the last about a mile long. Wheat ripe. Spent all but 25¢ for my supper and will have to remain over one train in order to sell some of my gold dust. Reached Cincinnatti at 12:30 A.M. Having breakfasted in Missouri, lunched in Illinois, dinned in Indiana and supped in Ohio. Stopped at the Burnett House.

CINCINNATTI, JUNE 19, 1867

Up at 7 o'clock. Breakfast not very good. I find that the Burnett approaches 2nd class in style. After breakfast spent my last 25¢ to get my boots blacked after which I took a vigorous walk one and one half hours duration about the north and east quarters of the city. Visited especially the suspension bridge across the Ohio, a noble work built by the same architect who built the one over Niagara, after which I returned to the hotel to await the opening of the Banks at 10 o'clock that I might sell some gold dust. At two I started out but found that the banks did not deal in the article. After much difficulty I found a jeweler who took 2 ounces at $21 per oz., after which I again rambled about the city, terminating my walk in the Washington Park, a place where the only points worthy of remark were a cool seat under the shade of the trees and some squirrels who gamboled about the park without the least fear of the people who were walking about. Visited the Cathedral, a beautifull building. Found the sexton absent from the Jewish synagogue and consequently could not enter. In the afternoon procured a ticket from the officers of the Spring Grove Cemetery Association, corner of Fourth and Walnut streets, and after dining at the Burnett House, I proceeded by three separate lines of street cars to the cemetery, which is about 4 miles from the Burnett House. At the entrance a beautifull little building has been built and an exact counterpart is being built with room enough for the entrance. It will be very tastefull when completed. At the intersection of two of the avenues in the cemetery, in a commanding postion, is placed a bronze statue by Rodgers representing a soldier on guard. Monuments poor but the grounds very fine and not as yet well arranged. At 8 o'clock I took a sleeping car on the Little Miami Railroad for Washington.[14]

ON THE CARS, JUNE 20, 1867

Awoke near Belaire. Breakfasted at the Ferry upon the boat while crossing the river, it being the first miserable meal I have had since leaving St. Louis. Here we leave Ohio and enter West Virginia. We have now rolling country. Very little level ground.

[14] The Little Miami, one of the earliest railroads in the United States, was built northward from Cincinnati to Springfield.

The R. R. runs through many tunnels along here, each ½ to ¾ of a mile in length. Passed along some coal ledges. I find the people here talking of the immorality of the "Mines" and congratulating themselves upon *their* worthyness—at the same time going to "The Black Crook" and laughing about it when it is the subject of conversation. Changed cars at junction for Washington.[15]

WASHINGTON, JUNE 21, 1867

First thing I saw in Washington was a tract society office with the windows dilapidated & broken. Stopped at Willards Hotel. Today I visited the Capitol, the Washington Monument, Patent Office, and Post Office. Dined at 5 P.M. after which I visited the Smithsonian Institution and in the evening went to see Ben Zoub Zoub Arab Jugglers. I was delighted with the Capitol Buildings. They consist of a centre building from which rises the dome and two wings, one on either side, each connected by a corridor with a new wing. The size of the centre building is, length 352 ft. 4 in. and width, including portico and steps, 290 ft. The dome which rises from the centre is 396½ ft. from the ground and 241 ft. above the top of the building, making the centre building 155½ feet high. The width of each of the two wings is 121 feet. This is what is called the old building and is built of yellow sandstone which has been painted white in order to preserve it and improve its looks. This part was finished in 1824 with the exception of the dome which has just been rebuilt in part. The two new wings which are connected with the old building by corridors 44 feet long and 56 ft. wide are very beautifull indeed, built of the finest white marble. The outside is a gem of beauty, while the inside is literally covered with marbles of beautifull colors from every part of the Union.

15 The latter part of Miller's diary and an additional account of his travels in Europe henceforth assume the character of a tourist's travelog. He is no longer describing a wilderness society, and the element of the primitively unknown, which characterized his western tour, was lost to him.

[Like any typical tourist, Miller was enthralled by Washington, whose patriotic shrines and artistic riches he had longed to see while on the wind-swept prairies and rock-girt mountains of the West. Alive with enthusiasm, he went from the capital to New York, reaching Manhattan on June 23, 1867. At Brooklyn he attentively listened to a lecture by the famous divine, Henry Ward Beecher. Miller left the gold dust which he had brought eastward at the Astor House and met W. H. Rockfellow, a relative of his Virginia City employer, who received him in very stiff, unwestern fashion. Together they deposited money belonging to John Rockfellow at the New York "Branch Mint" or "Assay Office," as Miller called it. Swindled by a hack driver, Miller again temporarily felt as lonely as when he had been out beyond the Rockies. He soon booked a second-class passage (for $100 in gold) on a French steamer, packed his mineral collection aboard, and sailed for Europe on June 29, 1867. The event was a moving one, and, as was customary with him, he described his feelings well: "As we passed the forts and slowly wound our way out to sea, and afterwards when the land slowly disappeared from sight, I felt a slight thumping in my heart as even to a matter-of-fact person the ocean is a wide gulf to separate one from his friends." Miller's first western tour was now finally over, and new adventures lay ahead.]

INDEX